f

SIZZLERS

The hate crime that
tore Sea Point apart

NICOLE ENGELBRECHT

mf

Melinda Ferguson Books,
an imprint of NB Publishers, a division of Media24 Boeke (Pty) Ltd
40 Heerengracht, Cape Town, South Africa
PO Box 879, Cape Town 8000, South Africa
www.nb.co.za

Cover design and typography: Wilna Combrinck
Editors: Melinda Ferguson
Proofreader: Riaan Wolmarans
Set in Sabon LT Pro
Printed and bound by CTP Printers, Cape Town

First published by Melinda Ferguson Books 2024
First edition, first impression

ISBN: 978-1-990973-82-6 (Print)
ISBN: 978-1-990973-83-3 (ePub)

Dedication

In memory of the nine young men who lost their lives in the crime dubbed the "Sizzlers massacre". You are our brothers, our sons, our friends and our partners. You are not forgotten.

Timothy Boyd
Sergio de Castro
Stephanus Fouché
Johan Meyer
Marius Meyer
Travis Reade
Warren Visser
Gregory Berghaus
Aubrey Otgaar

Contents

Dedication   5

Author's note   11

Blood   15

Aubrey & Sergio   21

Stephanus & Johan   31

Gregory & Travis   37

Timothy, Marius & Warren   42

First responders   49

The detective   55

Eyewitnesses   60

The survivor   65

The net closes   75

Trevor Theys   80

The interview   86

The first confession   90

Woest   97

Confession two   103

Three versions, one truth   108

My fiancé, the mass murderer   117

The journalists   121

The law of necessity   129

On trial   135

Justice?   143

Life for a life   148

Murder en masse   157

Killer friends   166

Scars   171

Treading water   177

The Van Wyk loophole   182

Where are the victims?   188

Navigating the system   194

Just say you're sorry   198

The sex worker   205

Hate crime, robbery or deadly message?   210

The present   223

Epilogue   229

Acknowledgments   231

Additional information   233

Sources   245

Author's note

Writing this book has been a delicate exercise in balance. With every piece of true-crime content I create, the victims are my most important focus. This time, I have been fortunate enough to have some of the victims' family members work with me and support the project. I considered them with every line I wrote. What would they think about this statement I'm making, this part that I'm describing? Would it make their huge pain and trauma even more unbearable, or would it help in some small way?

With 10 direct victims and countless secondary and tertiary victims, there is no way every person affected by the Sizzlers case will support or even like this book. I would never expect that. If you lost a loved one in the Sizzlers massacre, please know that I wrote this book with the greatest respect for you and the other victims. I may describe injuries, but not for salacious value: one of my major goals is to remind the South African public about the genuine horror of this crime. It's even more important now that one of the offenders is being considered for parole.

There are few ways left for us to honour these victims, but never forgetting what they endured in those three hours on 20 January 2003 is one of those ways. Another is to use the facts of this case to better understand the South African legal system, the parole system and the challenges faced by those who have lost loved ones to violent crime.

Twenty-one years later, contacting anyone related to the Sizzlers massacre has been extremely challenging. I have done my best to contact every person directly affected by this heinous crime. Some attempts have been unsuccessful; others agreed to contribute; and a few declined to take part. I had hoped to share a lot more information about the victims' lives as loved and cherished human beings. It pains me to have so little background on some of the men who were killed that night. I understand there are families who prefer not to go back to that time, and they honour their loved ones in their own ways.

The balancing act in this project did not relate only to the crimes' gruesomeness. There are other emotive and highly charged elements that, although difficult to confront, need to be discussed. Sizzlers was a sex-work establishment for individuals who wanted to engage in male-to-male massage and sex acts. We cannot look away from that, nor should we. The LGBTQ+ community was deeply scarred by this crime. Once more, sex workers were reminded of the perilous nature of their work and how unprotected they were by legislation at the time. In exploring these elements, I hope only to bring the light of truth to a case mired in confusion, shame and conspiracy theories.

Twenty-one years ago, nine young men were lost to the world, and the life of a tenth was forever changed.

Questions remain unanswered. Conspiracies abound. Families have somehow fumbled through the pain of grief into the "new normal" that was thrust upon them. The two men found guilty of the crime have never told the truth. That is undeniable. Perhaps in this book we will find it – or some version thereof.

Nicole Engelbrecht

Chapter 1

Blood

The night air is cool against the man's skin as the taxi pulls up in front of the house and he opens the door. He leans over and pays the driver. He notices the time: 3.14am. There's a good chance the same driver will still be on call in an hour when he's finished with his appointment. It's late. Business is slowing down, and not many drivers remain on duty.

It's January 2003 in Sea Point, Cape Town. The tourists who packed the beaches, restaurants, bars and clubs have mostly returned home. Memories, fading sunburns and specks of golden beach sand are all that remain of their holidays in one of the Western Cape's most popular holiday destinations. Some of those tourists may have patronised the establishment at 7 Graham Road during their stay.

The taxi driver often drops off men at the nondescript white house in the wee hours of the morning. The passengers sometimes radiate anxiety in the back seat – shifting uneasily or checking their watches, a thin film of sweat on their upper lips. They almost always scan the street for inquiring eyes before getting out.

The paint on the house's once-burgundy roof peels in the sea air, and the tree-lined structure looks ridiculously normal beside its flamingo-pink bed-and-breakfast neighbour. That's Sea Point for you: a diverse mix of people and tastes, with a dark underbelly that only some will acknowledge.

The taxi driver has learned to look the other way. His discretion, particularly in the early hours, is often rewarded with generous tips. In his experience, nothing good happens after midnight. That's when people let their darker sides come out to play. He nods at his latest client as the man gets out and shuts the door. The taxi leaves a puff of exhaust fumes in its wake.

Mark Hamilton is no stranger to Sizzlers massage parlour. He knows the owner, Aubrey Otgaar, who goes by "Eric". Many of the young men who work at Sizzlers are familiar too, although they often work there for only a few weeks.

Eric runs a tight ship. He's fair and somewhat of a father figure to the young men who work for him, but they know they're there to provide a service. Whether the government of South Africa views that service as legal is of no consequence. Eric expects professionalism: no drugs and alcohol while you're on duty. The faces at Sizzlers change fairly regularly, which doesn't surprise Hamilton – not all the men who have worked there over the years stuck to the rules, and many saw it as just a temporary way to make quick money. Eric's rules for his business are consistent, though, and that includes security. He is concerned not only about possible robberies or break-ins, but also about the people in the neighbourhood who have taken exception to him providing a service to gay men. Illogical hatred and homophobia can often be more dangerous than greed.

Hamilton is well aware of Eric's safety concerns, which is why he pauses when he sees the house's pedestrian gate standing open. The streetlight across the road doesn't offer enough illumination for him to notice that he's stepping in drops of blood as he slowly makes his way up the path to the house. The front door is open too. His breath hitches in his throat as he becomes aware of a strange smell. The door's hinges protest audibly as he steps inside the house, breaking an eerie silence. The house is usually a buzz of conversation and male laughter. He can hear the muffled drone of a television in the lounge. The workers gather around it at night until a client arrives. Then, the young man who has been booked – or selected on the spot – by the client heads off into one of the studios, and the rest keep watching whatever's on the screen.

The horrors that Hamilton encounters are too much for him to process all at once. In the passage, he finds the first sign that something extremely bad has occurred. On a half-moon imbuia table, next to a decorative bust of a bald figure carved from dark wood, a jewellery box and other trinkets, lies a knife. The blade is stained with drying blood. At the sight of the blood, Hamilton realises what he has been smelling. He has already identified the odour of petrol, which by itself made no sense, but the other sweet, metallic smell has evaded him – until now. Soon, he will see the source.

The first door on the left leads to the bedroom where the employees sleep. It is usually locked and used only on the odd occasion when the client rooms are all occupied. Tonight, it stands wide open, providing no barrier to the horror that lies within.

Hamilton will later say that although his eyes saw the bodies on the floor, he couldn't quite process the detail. He knew that something terrible had happened, but a kind of protection mechanism clicked on in his brain and wouldn't allow him to fully comprehend the gore around him.

He proceeds to the second room off the passage. This one, he knows from experience, is used for clients. He finds a man on the floor – bound, with brown packing tape stuck across his mouth and a pool of dark red blood congealing around him. The protection mechanism in Hamilton's brain ceases functioning, and he flees.

The forecourt staff at the Total petrol station on Main Road are nodding off in their plastic chairs as they wait for customers to pull up to the pumps. A garbled call for help breaks the silence just after 3am.

It takes a moment for the attendants to understand what they are seeing. At first, they think the young man stumbling and then dragging himself towards them is drunk. Brawls ignited by alcohol are not uncommon in the area, and certainly not unusual at this time of the morning. As they approach the man, who has now come to rest on the concrete floor of the petrol station, they realise this is no case of common assault. The white male in his twenties has brown packing tape wrapped around his face, a large gash to his throat and blood pouring from his head.

The first officer to respond that morning is one Captain Naude. He arrives at the Total garage just as Mark Hamilton comes running around the corner, screaming hysterically for help. Hamilton sees the injured man on the ground and quickly puts the pieces together. He asks the officer to follow him to the scene of the crime. Someone calls an ambulance for the young man at the petrol station – who will later be identified as Quinton Taylor – while Naude drives around to 7 Graham Road. His will be the first set of trained eyes to assess the scene, yet even he will admit being overwhelmed by what he sees.

He enters the house at 3.45am. In the first room, bunk beds line the wall. The beds are dishevelled. The air is heavy with the smell of blood. It lingers over the bodies of seven white men lying face down on the ground. Their hands and feet are bound with white nylon rope. Each victim has a sock in his mouth with brown plastic tape wrapped around it. Naude checks the victims for signs of life. One or two may have a thready pulse.

In the next room, he discovers the eighth victim, lying on his side and also bound with white rope. He finds the last victim in the bathroom. The man is not bound but is deceased. Each victim has sustained throat and head wounds similar to Quinton Taylor's injuries. Of all the horrors Naude faces that night, it is the sound of garbled gasps for breath that stays with him.

When a person's throat is slit, the manner and speed of death depend on the location and depth of the incision. If a jugular vein or one of the carotid arteries on either side of the neck is severed, the victim can bleed out in minutes. If, instead, injury occurs to the trachea (the breathing tube), blood can flow down the tube and pool in the lungs. If the victim is still alive, each attempted breath may result in blood bubbling up in the trachea, producing a gurgling sound. This is what Naude will continue to hear in his head for some time to come.

He leaves the house and calls for several ambulances and backup vehicles. He waits outside, perhaps unwilling to contend with the horrors inside 7 Graham Road on his own. One look has been enough. The smells, sounds and horrendous visuals are etched into his brain.

Chapter 2

Aubrey & Sergio

Aubrey

Aubrey John Otgaar, who went by the name "Eric" for business purposes, was born on 15 January 1947. He was 56 years old at the time of his death. Sadly, he hadn't intended to stay in South Africa for much longer. He had connected online with a man who lived in Eastern Europe and told friends that, in less than a month, he would go there – and, if things went well, stay there for a while.

He never got the opportunity to see if his digital romance held any promise.

Aubrey's former partner and friend describes him as a bit of a joker who enjoyed playing clever pranks on people. His family recalls one prank spread out over several weeks at his grandmother's house. The young Aubrey had planted stink bombs in strategic places all over the house. Whenever his grandmother unwittingly set one off, she would blame the dog's flatulence. This went on for some time until she was ready to take the dog to the vet, certain that the poor animal had a terrible stomach complaint.

Aubrey had been openly gay for much of his adult life. This, along with his decision to work in the sex trade, had at times put a strain on his relationship with his devoutly Catholic family. At Aubrey's funeral, his younger brother Tony recalled that he had set aside his own biases and reconciled with his brother just two years earlier. After the events of 20 January 2003, he was unendingly grateful that he had. Who knows what his grief would have been like if his brother had been murdered while they were still at odds?

Unapologetic about his place and choices in the world, Aubrey had also wanted to make a difference in a legal context. In the late 1970s and early 1980s, he had been a member of the Progressive Party. At the time, the party represented the legal opposition to apartheid within South Africa's white minority. Of his brother's sense of social responsibility, Tony said: "He was vocal in his criticism of the government when they failed in the area of corruption and the safety of its citizens, and [he] was also critical of the government's Aids policy. He was transparent and, as a family, we differed on the nature of his work. But we remained close-knit."

Unlike many owners of sex-trade establishments who do not have the best of reputations and fall victim to the temptations of fast money, drugs and illicit sex, Aubrey was well-respected. Sex workers are vulnerable. Their trade is still illegal, and many owners abuse this vulnerability because they know their workers don't have much recourse. By all accounts, Aubrey was not like that.

A young man who attended his funeral but preferred not to be identified said he had worked for Aubrey for a few months and had only good things to say. Although he eventually decided that sex work wasn't for him, he had grown as a person because Aubrey had created a supportive environment where he hadn't had to hide his sexual orientation. Aubrey had always encouraged him to be proud of who he was, in all respects.

Debbie Williams (not her real name) met Aubrey when they were both in their teens, living in Port Elizabeth (now Gqeberha). They were close friends throughout their lives, although their paths would sometimes go in opposite directions before converging again.

One of these convergences came in the late 1990s, when Aubrey lived in Sea Point and Debbie was in nearby Mouille Point. She had always known that Aubrey was gay. In fact, she says, she doesn't recall him telling her – it was just part of who he was. The pair spent many nights in Sea Point's gay clubs and bars. She recalls with a smile how Aubrey was often the centre of attention. One night, after a few too many drinks, they "permanently borrowed" a rainbow flag from the wall of one of the bars. Aubrey hung it over his bed, and they giggled about it every time she visited his home.

Debbie also says she had always known that Aubrey worked in the sex trade. When he felt he was no longer young and fit enough to work himself, he turned his hand to running Sizzlers. Debbie visited the house on Graham Road many times. At first, she says, the workers weren't living there. "It was just an ordinary home," she says. "He actually ran the business by having his driver drop the workers off at hotels or clients' homes. They didn't come to his house at all in the beginning."

But then, something changed. Twenty-one years later, she's still not certain what it was, but Aubrey seemed desperate. He was jumpy and anxious. When she asked him what was wrong, he just smiled ruefully and said, "Business is tough." He then moved the bunk beds into the house, and the workers started living there.

"It seemed to boost his income, having the men staying there," Debbie says, "but I didn't like it. I told him it was dangerous."

Aubrey also increased his working hours. "At first, he ran it like a nine-to-five and didn't even answer the phone after hours."

After the workers moved in, though, Sizzlers was open 24/7. "It made it difficult for him to have any friends over," Debbie recalls. "The clients didn't really want to see a bunch of people hanging around because they were concerned for their privacy." So, Debbie stopped visiting, and soon she and Aubrey were hardly speaking.

"I was walking in Sea Point a few weeks before the massacre happened, and I saw Aubrey sitting at an outside table at a bar." Her face darkens as she recalls the day. "He was wearing makeup – he did that sometimes, just because he liked it – but it was smudged all down his face and he looked terrible."

Debbie didn't stop to speak to her old friend that night because she was with other friends and didn't want to intrude. Not long after, a shared acquaintance phoned her to tell her that Aubrey had been murdered.

"My first thought, after I got over the shock, was for his

dogs." A fact not featured in any reports on the Sizzlers massacre was that Aubrey's two miniature poodles had lived in the house with him. Debbie says they had been in the house on the night of the massacre. They were found cowering under his bed almost 48 hours later. She heard the dogs were later adopted.

"He was a huge dog lover," Debbie says. "He actually bred the poodles at one stage, and I got a puppy from him." She proudly displays a picture on her phone of a white ball of fluff called Toby.

She hardly ever talks about Aubrey anymore, she says, but she has looked at old photographs of him. She also has a video of part of his funeral. "A bit of a weird thing to keep, I guess," she shrugs. "I don't feel like it's something I can just put in the bin, though."

As she talks, she realises how many memories of that time she has repressed – or perhaps she never has an opportunity to talk about it anymore. "It's not like you can just bring up something like this at the dinner table, you know?"

It feels good, though, she says, to talk about him again. For a long time, she felt angry about how his life was snatched away, but now she just feels sad that he didn't live to be in his 70s like her. "He was a good man. I miss him."

Aubrey Otgaar was laid to rest after a service at St Anthony's Catholic Church in Belmont Park. His coffin – draped in purple cloth, one of his favourite colours – was topped with bunches of white flowers. The aesthetic of the scene belied the horror of what the unapologetically out and open joker had experienced in his last hours on earth.

℮

On 21 January 2003, forensic pathologists Dr Lorna Martin and Dr Denise Lourens performed an autopsy on the body of Aubrey John Otgaar (death register 151/2003). They found that he had sustained two perforating gunshot wounds to the back of his head. As the bullets moved through his brain, they fractured his skull, causing subarachnoid bleeding over the surface of his brain. The exit points were just above his left forehead.

The doctors observed a large, gaping incision on the left side of Aubrey's neck. It had cut through his neck muscles, carotid artery and pharynx. He had a ligature abrasion on his right wrist, multiple contusions on his upper arms and a contusion consistent with a human bite mark on his right shoulder. The cause of his death was the gunshot wounds to his head.

Sergio

At 22 years old, Sergio de Castro was one of the youngest victims of the massacre. The lean, dark-haired young man with a dazzling smile was charming, loving and generous, according to his friends.

Born and raised in Johannesburg, Sergio worked in a Joburg nightclub before moving to Cape Town in 2000. Seeking community, he joined the 11-member choir at St Mary's Cathedral upon his arrival in Sea Point. The choir director, Stephen Wrankmore, said Sergio was a tenor but had dreams of becoming a cantor and performing solo pieces. He soon saw that the young man was determined: he didn't have a car, but he always made a plan to get to choir practice.

It appears that none of Sergio's friends in Cape Town had known that he was working at Sizzlers. Terry Casper met Sergio when he was dating a friend of hers. She says he was a beautiful soul who was always surprised when someone did something for him, despite his willingness to give endlessly to others. When Sergio and his partner briefly shared a flat with almost no furniture, Terry gave them some of her old pieces. Sergio was shocked that she didn't want anything in return.

One of Sergio's friends went through his belongings after his death and discovered that he had completed a certificate in web development but owed R13,000 in tuition fees. The amount had to be paid before he could receive his certificate and start applying for jobs. Many believe that his stint at Sizzlers was a way of raising that money – a temporary solution for a more promising future that never came to pass.

Before Sizzlers, Sergio had worked at a coffee shop, but the money wasn't enough to get him to his goal. He looked for additional work at laundromats and other businesses, seemingly happy to work two or three jobs simultaneously to pay for his tuition. But, even so, it would have taken far too long to save up R13,000, which was a lot of money back in 2000. (Lucrative instant returns are often part of the allure of sex work.)

Mario de Biaisio had befriended Sergio when they met at St Mary's Cathedral not long after the young man first arrived in Sea Point. He says that Sergio shared some details of his childhood with him.

Sergio was born to a Portuguese mother and an Afrikaans father. His mother had left him with his father when he was three years old, he said, and he had no further contact with her. When he was seven, his father died and he was moved between members of his extended family and, eventually, foster homes until he was old enough to live on his own. At the time of his death, Sergio's only surviving immediate family member was his 16-year-old half-brother. Mario had to identify Sergio's body in the mortuary.

As is often the case, there are conflicting stories about the latter part of Sergio's life. After his death, his former partner, Eugene Havemann, told journalists that Sergio's foray into sex work had started while he was still living in Johannesburg. Apparently, he went to Cape Town to start afresh by working as a web developer, but perhaps the allure of the quick money he could earn at Sizzlers was too strong.

Eugene met Sergio when the young man was still living in a foster home. He claimed the family was abusing him, and Eugene, who was 23 at the time, approached the courts to get permission for the then-17-year-old to live with him. Their relationship blossomed into a romance after Sergio turned 18, Eugene says. Sergio always seemed to be searching for something, though – and Eugene came home one day to find he had moved out. The next he heard of Sergio was the news of his death.

Sometime after Sergio's murder, his mother watched a television documentary about the case. Although she hadn't seen her son in many years, hearing his name and seeing his face got her attention.

The woman said she had left her husband when Sergio was three years old but insisted that she had maintained contact with her son. She admitted that Sergio never lived with her again but said he had visited her at her house when he was 10 years old.

She would later claim she had not intended to abandon her son, and that their separation had been due to a contentious divorce. Sergio's father remarried about four years after their divorce, and she said his new wife didn't want her to have contact with her son. All anecdotal evidence available confirms, though, that Sergio's father died when he was seven. If his mother saw him when he was 10, the boy would already have been living with family members and in foster homes. She said she had longed for her son every day, and she was devastated to hear he'd thought she had abandoned him – and that he was now dead.

Stephen Wrankmore, the choir director, said Sergio had a wonderful sense of humour and lived life on his own terms.

"He would sometimes arrive for Mass looking very smart in a beautiful leather jacket and then, another time, he would wear a swimming suit and a sarong. He was a fantastic person, and it hurts me very much that he is gone and that so many people will not know him for who he really was – that people will just remember him as a victim of this terrible event."

The event was indeed terrible, and the injuries inflicted upon the defenceless young man even more so.

Sergio's autopsy was the first to be conducted on 21 January 2003. The death register number was 149/2003. The pathologists observed a perforating gunshot wound to Sergio's head, the track of which ran through his brain, causing subdural and subarachnoid bleeding before exiting above his right ear. The left side of his neck had been slashed, with his neck muscles incised, but nothing deeper than that. There were ligature abrasions on his left wrist and both ankles. The cause of his death was the gunshot wound.

Chapter 3

Stephanus & Johan

Stephanus

Many of the young men who lost their lives at Sizzlers used pseudonyms to protect their identities. This is not uncommon in the sex trade, as clients can become obsessed with sex workers and try to track them down outside their workplace. In addition, many do this to keep their family members from finding out they work in the sex trade. As a result, it's difficult to know how the victims preferred to be known. This is the case with the youngest victim of the massacre.

The 17-year-old who went by "Ryan" was christened Stephanus Abraham Fouché when he was adopted by Fanus and Anita Fouché. His dad called him Fanie. The family lived a simple but comfortable life in Theunissen in the Free State. Fanus worked as a boilermaker and his wife was a homemaker. When the couple realised they could not have children, they decided to adopt instead – and Stephanus came into their lives as an infant.

Fanus said that his son had always been responsible and more mature than his peers. So, when Stephanus said he wanted to leave home and venture into the world on his own, his father didn't want to stand in his way. Stephanus had completed grade 10 and, although his parents would have preferred that he finish school, he had his mind set on a future in Cape Town.

"One day he said, 'Dad, I want to go to Cape Town.' I couldn't stop him. We kept in touch, but we didn't know what he was doing. We thought he was working in computers."

Stephanus was an only child, so it was difficult for his parents to let him go. They consoled themselves with knowing he'd be back for Christmas and other holidays. Stephanus did go home for Christmas in 2002. He spent a blissful two weeks in the Free State before returning to Sea Point. Twenty days later, his parents got the call to say there would be no more Christmases with Stephanus.

His mom, Anita, had spoken to her son on the night of the massacre. Nothing in their conversation had given her any inkling of what lay ahead.

The Fouchés first heard that something bad had happened from a neighbour who had seen the news coverage of the Sizzlers massacre and knew that their son lived in Sea Point. At first, they did not know what to think. There were rumours that the house was a venue for sex work, but it was the same address their son had given them as his residence. Finally, unable to get hold of their boy, Fanus got in his bakkie and drove to Cape Town. He returned five days later with Stephanus's body in the back of the bakkie.

For a long time, Stephanus's dad chose to believe that his son had been at 7 Graham Road that night to repair the computers. After all, this is how his son had said he was earning his keep. He had always been talented with computers, and his friends joked that he could disassemble and reassemble a computer faster than most people could cook dinner. In a later interview, Fanus told a reporter that he didn't care that his son had been employed at Sizzlers as a sex worker. He had always been immensely proud of his child, and nothing would change that.

An emotional Fanus told the reporter, "I want to tell the world that I am proud of my son. He was the most beautiful boy. He could look anyone straight in the eye and say, 'I am Fanie Fouché.' He was proud. He spoke the truth. I want to tell the whole of South Africa that he was the best kid."

Stephanus's murder brings a new element into this case. At eight months shy of his 18th birthday, he was a minor. A young man who had worked with Stephanus until just before his death (and who thankfully was absent on the night of the murders) said that Stephanus had admitted to him that he was under 18. To clients and anyone else who asked, Stephanus was 19. The young man did not know whether Aubrey had been aware of Stephanus's real age – but one would think a man described as a stickler for rules would have asked the young men he hired for proof of age. Fake IDs are not impossible to come by, though. Under different circumstances, someone would have been held to account for a minor's presence in a sex establishment, but at Sizzlers, there was no one left to blame.

Yet, some said the victims themselves were to blame. They

had allegedly been engaging in some form of sex work and were gay to boot! What had they thought would happen? It is an argument no less ridiculous or insulting than asking a female rape victim why she had worn a miniskirt.

While Sergio de Castro's funeral was taking place in St Mary's Cathedral, 1,000 kilometres away, the Fouchés and their friends, neighbours and family members gathered to bid farewell to Stephanus. He was buried out of the Dutch Reformed Church. Dominee Hans Griesel led the gathered mourners in prayer and reminded them of the church's view of the rumours swirling around Stephanus's murder. "Let the short life of Fanie call us all to look at our own lives. It is through the dead that we are all called to lead a Christian life in this heartbroken world."

Fanie Fouché's response was unwavering support of his son. "I wish that everybody who wants to throw a stone must throw a stone at me – and I will show to them that you can't throw a stone unless you are blameless."

Stephanus's funeral ended in much the same way that Sergio's had – with flowers on a wooden box containing all that remained of a young man's hopes and dreams. This time, the flowers were white petals, cast from the hands of his grieving parents. More beauty and more horror.

Stephanus's autopsy was the fourth conducted on the day after the murders. The death register number was 154/2003.

The findings were short and simple. The pathologists acknowledged his legal status as a juvenile. A single gunshot wound had penetrated the back of his head, but there was no sign of an exit wound. The gunshot track had resulted in significant injury to his brain. There were penetrating incised wounds visible on his neck, but these were mostly superficial.

Johan

Like many of the other young men working at Sizzlers, 22-year-old Johan Joseph Meyer was not a born-and-bred Capetonian. He was raised in Johannesburg in a low-income family and moved to Cape Town to look for work. His parents hadn't known the nature of his job at Sizzlers.

Johan's parents were, of course, devastated and faced the added challenge of lacking the means to travel to Cape Town. Worse still, they had no idea how they would get their son's body back to Johannesburg for burial. Unlike Stephanus's dad, who at least had his own bakkie to transport his son's remains, the Meyers had no transport and no money.

When this was reported in the media, Winnie Madikizela-Mandela, the former wife of Nelson Mandela, offered to help pay for the couple to travel to Cape Town and take their son's body home. The Meyers gratefully accepted the offer, and Johan returned home for the last time.

❧

Johan Meyer is the only victim whose autopsy report was not included in the released paperwork and could not be located. The error may have slipped in because there was another victim with the same surname. Undoubtedly, though, his autopsy results would have been similar to those of the other victims: a penetrating gunshot to the head and either superficial or penetrating incised wounds to the neck.

Chapter 4

Gregory & Travis

Gregory

Forty-three-year-old Gregory Seymour Berghaus was the only victim not employed by Sizzlers. He was at the house as a client, and was believed to be engaged in an appointment with one of the sex workers when the massacre occurred.

Gregory was born on 30 October 1959 and had strong bonds with his mother and two siblings. Exceptionally intelligent, he obtained two degrees in South Africa and quickly advanced in his career as an extremely successful prop stylist and antique collector. His work appeared in high-end international magazines, and his mother, Fay, said that her son had an "exceptional eye for beauty".

His friends described him as an "extraordinary man" who could make anyone feel like the most special person in the room. He had moved to New York 15 years before the massacre and, at the time of his death, was still officially living there. He was in Cape Town for the festive season to visit his family. Some of his friends said he had been considering moving back to South Africa permanently, but at that point, the visit to Sizzlers was just part of his holiday. Sadly, it would be a fatal decision.

Gregory did not die immediately from his injuries that night and, along with two other victims, was rushed to Groote Schuur Hospital. His mother, his sister, Shelley, and his brother, Eugene, spent the next four days at his bedside, praying for his survival. Unfortunately, his injuries were too severe and he died in hospital. He was laid to rest in the Jewish section of Pinelands Cemetery.

Gregory Berghaus' autopsy was carried out on 25 January 2003. His death register number was 192/2003. Dr Lorna Martin found that he had sustained a perforating gunshot wound to his left temple, and the bullet had exited at the back of his head. The bullet track ran through the left part of his cerebrum, where his brain tissue had started dying off. Doctors had conducted a craniotomy on him to alleviate the pressure on his brain caused by the bleeding and to minimise brain damage.

Gregory was different from the other victims in many ways, and so was his autopsy. Besides being one of the three victims who were taken to hospital, Gregory was also the only victim with an additional gunshot wound elsewhere on his body. Martin noted that he had sustained a penetrating gunshot wound to the abdomen, which had lacerated his small bowel and appendix. He had the same incised wound to his neck as the other victims, but it had been sutured at the hospital. He had ligature marks around his wrists. The gunshot wound and its consequences were the cause of his death.

Travis

Twenty-year-old Travis Reade went by the name "Max" at work. Hailing from Johannesburg, he too had come to Cape Town with the belief that it would improve his life. He had been in the city for three years when he was killed at Sizzlers.

Travis's father, Len, had suspected that his son worked in the sex trade and did not approve, although Travis never admitted it. Len said he believed his son had been a sex worker for the entire three years he had been in Cape Town. This means that Travis, like Stephanus, started in the sex trade when he was still a minor.

Len thought that his son had worked at Sizzlers the whole time, but there is no concrete proof of this. He said it had been extremely difficult to keep track of his son. He'd regularly changed his cellphone number, and Len had spoken to him only a handful of times while he lived in Cape Town. However, he had convinced Travis to come home for a visit in September 2002, and they had enjoyed each other's company. He had no idea how valuable their time together would seem by January the following year.

Travis's friends said he had lived life on his own terms and seen his time at Sizzlers as a means to an end. He was young and attractive, and he told his friends he'd make the most of that while he could. Travis enjoyed spending the money he earned and was never short of expensive clothes, jewellery and gadgets. Len also suspected that his son had developed a drug habit that kept him trapped in the sex trade.

Travis's parents had divorced when he was relatively young, and his mother, Alison Fleishman, had remarried. When she and Len were informed of their son's murder, their worlds came crashing down.

Len's sister lived in Cape Town, and she had the horrific duty of identifying Travis's body. He was one of the first to be identified, so she also had to see some of the other victims' bodies before they found Travis.

For years, Alison was haunted by what her son went through in his last minutes on earth. She felt guilty for not protecting him and couldn't picture him without his injuries for a very long time.

In the days after Travis's murder, his father told reporters that he wanted to set up a fund to help male prostitutes get out of the industry. He felt it might allow some good to come from his son's senseless death.

Travis Reade was allocated the death register number 153/2003. His autopsy was conducted on 22 January 2003, the second day of autopsies after the massacre. Dr Denise Lourens noted that Travis had sustained a gunshot wound to the left side of his head with a wound tract that involved the brain but with no exit wound. He had superficial cuts to his neck. One of the most tragic notations in the autopsy was that Travis had aspirated the contents of his stomach. It is highly probable that the young man vomited due to being forced to lie on his stomach in a state of terror. His attackers had placed a sock in his mouth and taped it over to keep it in place. This was done to silence him, but when Travis vomited, it also meant that his stomach contents had nowhere to go. He choked and inhaled his own vomit. The cause of death was the gunshot wound to his head.

Chapter 5

Timothy, Marius & Warren

Timothy

Timothy Craig Boyd was 29 years old when he was murdered in the massacre at Sizzlers. Another Johannesburg transplant, he had also lived in KwaZulu-Natal as a child.

The oldest among the sex workers, Timothy hadn't been working at Sizzlers for long. He had been in the sex industry for much of his twenties. Before Sizzlers, he had worked at another male-escort establishment in Sea Point for six months. Timothy had already informed his friends that he was planning to exit the industry. It was time for him to move on to a new phase of his life. But his fresh start would never come.

Timothy's friends said he had regularly phoned his parents but not spoken about his family much, and no one was sure whether they'd known what work he did. A young woman who had been dating Timothy for a few months before his death spoke to a journalist in the weeks after the massacre. He was one of the last to be identified and, although she had suspected he was among the victims, she had to wait nine days for confirmation.

The journalist assigned her the pseudonym "Roxanne Andrews". She, too, had been involved in the sex trade at one point and didn't want to use her real name. Roxanne said she and Timothy had been in a relationship for about four months, and she'd ended it when she discovered he was lying to her about his job. She believed he had been planning to get out of the trade soon, and that's perhaps why he didn't admit to his sex work, but she couldn't look past the deception.

She described their relationship as "wonderful", saying Timothy had treated her well and every other aspect of their relationship had been perfect. He hadn't spoken about his parents much, but she knew he had been close to his sister and niece.

On the night of the massacre, Timothy had phoned one of Roxanne's friends and made plans to go to a club after his shift at Sizzlers ended. Their 2am meeting never happened, and they discovered the terrible reason the next day.

Roxanne had extracted herself from the sex trade and was working in tourism at the time of Timothy's death. From her own experience, she had been concerned he wouldn't make it out because he was spending money "like water". He used cocaine occasionally and, in her opinion, did not seem to have what it would take to get out. Timothy often spoke of wanting to start a family with someone one day. The massacre snatched away that dream.

Timothy Boyd's autopsy was conducted on the first day of autopsies for the victims of the massacre. His death register number was 150/2003. Dr Lorna Martin noted a single perforating gunshot wound: the bullet had entered the back of Timothy's head and exited out his right eye, causing damage to his brain and subdural and subarachnoid bleeding. The incised wounds to Timothy's neck differed from those of the other victims. Rather than slicing, his attackers had stabbed him in the neck three time, cutting through his neck muscles. He had ligature abrasions on both of his ankles and on his right wrist.

Marius

Twenty-one-year-old Marius Meyer was born and raised in Barkly West in the Northern Cape. He had allegedly entered the sex trade when he could not find other employment.

Marius was one of the victims who survived long enough to be transported to Groote Schuur Hospital for treatment. He succumbed to his injuries not long after arriving there.

After his murder, his mother told journalists she didn't want to speak about her son, but added: "People can say and think what they want, but he was a good person." She and many other parents also told journalists at the time that they had been instructed by police not to talk to the media. Her husband drove to Cape Town to identify his son and arrange for his body to be transported back home.

There is almost no information available about Marius's

life. His parents still live in Barkly West and own a business there. Like many of the other victims' families, they have their own ways of remembering their son and prefer not to speak publicly about him.

⁂

Marius's autopsy took place on 22 January 2003. Dr Lorna Martin mentioned in her report that he had sustained a perforating gunshot wound to his left temple. The bullet track had caused subdural and subarachnoid haemorrhaging in the brain and swelling. The bullet had exited through his right temple. Marius had three incised wounds to his neck, which had cut into his neck muscles and were sutured at the hospital. He also had ligature abrasions on his ankles. The cause of death was the gunshot wound to his head.

Warren

Warren Robert Visser was just 22 years old when he was murdered. He was a qualified computer technician and had plans to start his master's in the field. However, he struggled to find employment and, as a result, had been working at Sizzlers for a month when the massacre occurred.

Warren's family was religious, and he had been an altar boy in his childhood. His parents held a dim view of his decision to work at Sizzlers, but his mom, Marlene, still tried to keep in regular contact with her son although she says he often dodged her phone calls. He'd grown up with two siblings, a younger brother and sister. His sister, Leigh, was just 14 years old when she received the news of her brother's death.

Marlene described her son as kind, compassionate and intelligent, with a beautiful soul. He loved to laugh and enjoyed spending time with people. Warren was also a prankster, and Marlene has many cherished memories – especially of Warren teasing Leigh.

Leigh remembers her brother fondly. She was the baby of the family and the only girl, and Warren often played dolls with her. As her older brother, he was protective. One memory stands out for her as an apt representation of who her brother was. Leigh had some pocket money and wanted to spend it on sweets, so Warren offered to walk her to the shop. On the way, two men were walking behind them, swearing in conversation and telling each other dirty jokes. Warren stopped and turned to the men, saying, "Excuse me, can you see I am walking with a young lady here?" That exemplified Warren. He knew right from wrong and wasn't afraid to stand up for what was right.

Many of Leigh's favourite childhood memories involve Warren. Her other brother is just 10 months older than Leigh, but Warren's playful nature meant he often had the family in stitches. He would dress up in ridiculous outfits, Leigh says, just to make her laugh.

On Sunday 19 January 2003, the Visser family watched the Sunday-night movie. Leigh recalls going to bed later that night thinking that she was the luckiest girl in the world. She had a warm and safe home and a loving family, and it felt like nothing in the world could disturb their perfect cocoon. In just four hours, all of that would change forever.

Leigh awoke to the hysterical screams of her mother, Marlene. In a horrible twist of fate, the power had tripped during the night. Once it was restored, the television turned on by itself. The Vissers did not usually watch the morning news on a weekday, but early on Monday, Marlene went to switch off the television while the news was on. It took her just a few moments to understand what she was seeing.

When she heard her mom screaming, "Oh my God, Warren is dead, Warren is dead!", Leigh's first thought was that her mom was exaggerating. Chaos ensued. Marlene called her husband, Leigh's stepfather, to come home from work, and Leigh remembers the adults making lots of telephone calls. Eventually, her stepfather went to the mortuary to see if Warren was there. He wasn't. This gave the family some hope, but still Marlene felt something terrible had happened. Soon, a news update gave them glimmer of promise – some survivors had made it to the hospital.

Leigh recalls retreating to her bedroom that day. She listened to radio news updates about what had happened at Sizzlers while her mother phoned around, trying to find Warren. "Then they announced one survivor had just passed away in the hospital, and I remember feeling … I don't know how I knew … but I was like, 'That's my brother.'"

Leigh's intuition was right. As the teenager sat in her bedroom, her world turned from perfect to horrific overnight as her big brother's body succumbed to the horrific injuries inflicted upon him by his attackers.

Dr Lorna Martin conducted Warren Visser's autopsy on 22 January 2003. Leigh's big brother and protector was issued death register number 159/2003.

The doctor observed a perforating gunshot wound to Warren's right temple. The bullet had exited through his left scalp. The bullet track had damaged Warren's brain and caused subdural and subarachnoid bleeding. There were three incised wounds, which had been sutured at the hospital. One of these had entered through the right posterior chest cavity. There were ligature marks on his wrists and ankles. The gunshot wound to his head was the cause of death.

Chapter 6

First responders

In the early hours of 20 January 2003, emergency medicine specialist and advanced life-support paramedic Nick Nevin is off duty. At this time, he is the operations manager for Netcare 911 at Christiaan Barnard Memorial Hospital in Cape Town. He is not on duty because his emergency response vehicle's siren is not working. The vehicle cannot be used until it is repaired. But what happens at 7 Graham Road in Sea Point that morning changes everything. The rules will no longer apply after one of Cape Town's biggest mass shootings on record.

The shrill call coming in awakens Nick. The other response unit is still a long way off, and they need all hands on deck. So, he decides to use his vehicle despite the siren not working. Given that it is still very early in the morning, he doesn't have to worry about traffic. The urgency of the situation outweighs the risk.

As Nick enters Sea Point, he spots the ambulance parked at the Total garage. He slows down and approaches one of the paramedics on the scene, thinking he might have the wrong address. They explain that only one victim is at the garage; the rest are at the house around the corner.

In Graham Road, police have already cordoned off the scene. Emergency vehicles line the street. Due to the smell of petrol in the house and the risk of ignition, they have also asked the fire department to attend. Other paramedic units and several police cars have arrived, so Nick parks about 150 metres from the house and carries his equipment in as quickly as possible.

The house is chaotic. Various first responders stand around, and a police officer points Nick to the first room on the left. There, he finds one of his colleagues already attending to a patient. In the rapid-fire exchange of information that he's accustomed to, his colleague tells him that the other victims in the room have already been declared dead. Only two young men are still clinging to life. Nick gets to work.

He assesses the victim and notes the gunshot wound and incision to the neck. His first action is to sedate the patient so that he can insert an airway into his lungs to help him breathe. Also, given the circumstances and the fear and potential pain the victims have experienced, sedation is a favourable option. The patient is breathing but hardly conscious; once the sedative has been administered, he will not be aware of anything happening around him.

Due to the chaotic environment and distant parking, the medics spend more time than usual on the scene. Managing head wounds is always difficult and time-sensitive, and Nick knows all too well that he needs to get his patient to the hospital if he's going to have a fighting chance.

Following traumatic head injuries, the brain starts to swell. Clinicians usually follow the "golden hour" rule to increase a patient's chances of recovery. Brain swelling quickly leads to brain damage, which, in turn, causes the rest of the patient's body to shut down.

Nick spends about 30 minutes at the scene, which is not ideal, but the nature of the call means anything less is impossible. Eventually, they transport the patients to Groote Schuur Hospital and hand them over to the emergency care team.

As the sun comes up, the paramedics gather on the trauma deck of the hospital to sort out their equipment. In the chaos of the mass-casualty event, everyone just grabbed what they needed from each other to save lives, and now they have to get their equipment back and clean it before their next calls.

Due to the pressure and the gruesome nature of the scene at Sizzlers, Nick and his colleagues had not realised the enormity of the situation. He'd never left the room where he was treating his patient, so he initially had no idea there were other victims too. Now, while rinsing off stretchers and sanitising their resuscitation equipment, the medics share snippets of what they experienced. They'll do a formal debrief later at Nick's suggestion as ops manager, but this is the first opportunity to discuss what they saw. Get it out, so it doesn't fester.

One of Nick's colleagues mentions that he was working on a patient in the bathroom. Others speculate about what could have taken place. There is a general sense of unease: they all saw something that will never leave them.

Nick arrives home later and shrugs off his jacket. He's

aware of a strange feeling stirring inside him, but it takes a moment for him to understand what it is. He's on edge – even in his own home. Despite all he's seen in the line of duty, what he witnessed at 7 Graham Road has robbed him of his feeling of personal safety. The unknown faces of the perpetrators haunt him. He thinks, "If an individual or more than one individual can go into a space and do the things that they did to those people, then none of us are safe."

Nick Nevin has significant experience in pre-hospital emergency medicine. He's lived and worked in Johannesburg and Cape Town, including at the Brixton Fire Department for a year after qualifying. He treated more gunshot wounds in that year than many medics will treat in their entire careers.

He describes the depth of his experience as "several lifetimes' worth of crime scenes". When he pulled up outside the house on Graham Road, though, everything changed. "As much as I was already well versed in the human being's factory settings, and the brutality that we are capable of, I had not yet seen it on the scale I witnessed in the early hours of that morning in January. And, although I have seen many brutal things since, Sizzlers still stands out from a scale perspective."

Nick struggles to put into words why this scene was so different from the rest and why it left him with such a deep sense of vulnerability. As the days and weeks passed after the murders, little pieces of the puzzle fell into place.

He had to go back to the scene a second time to walk

the forensic pathologist through the house and provide the emergency personnel's perspective. This helps the pathologist understand how the victims were originally positioned, which, in turn, can explain factors such as lividity (the bluish-purple discolouration of skin after death). In South Africa, it is rare for emergency personnel to be called out to conduct such a walkthrough with a forensic pathologist. It was the first time Nick had been asked to do so.

Although it would be ideal for a qualified forensic pathologist to attend the scene of every unnatural death, the sheer number of deaths in South Africa makes that impossible. Pretoria-based forensic pathologist Prof Ryan Blumenthal estimates that there are about 70,000 unnatural deaths in South Africa every year. Roughly 25,000 of these are ruled homicides. The Department of Health employs only between 60 and 70 qualified pathologists. The resources are clearly inadequate.

Even so, many cases have benefited from pathologists attending a murder scene. Their training helps them assess a scene differently from other attending personnel, and sometimes this aids in the conviction of a perpetrator. A pathologist's crime scene is the human body, but the environment in which that victim died also plays a role in determining the circumstances of their death. Many serial murderers' crimes are first linked by forensic pathologists, who may examine bodies from different police jurisdictions and notice the similarities in modus operandi before anyone else.

The Forensic Pathology Service is responsible for collecting the bodies of dead people in South Africa. Due to the lack of pathologists, staff members who transport bodies to mortuaries are trained in basic evidence collection and protection. This includes "bagging" a victim's hands to protect DNA evidence under their fingernails.

A forensic pathologist is only called to the scene when the police can see a case will be complex or where the victim's body presents specific types of evidence. The Sizzlers massacre was one such case. Mass murders attract media attention, and no one wants anything to slip through the cracks.

During his walkthrough, Nick Nevin begins to understand what had bothered him about the Sizzlers scene. He is used to blood and gory injuries, but the rooms at 7 Graham Road had been drenched in blood. "I mean, there was blood everywhere. There was blood on the floor, there was blood on the walls and there was blood on the ceiling, which is, you know, not something that you see often."

Although he didn't actively follow the case thereafter, he would hear bits and pieces as time went by – and the question of motive always bugged him. He had attended scenes where robberies had gone wrong, and knew what they looked like and what type of injuries he would find. Sizzlers was different. In his experience, the "protracted physical and psychological torture" was not indicative of a robbery gone wrong.

Nick is a logical man. He has the scientific mind of a medical professional, but the only way he can describe the Sizzlers massacre is to say, "It just felt like it was evil."

Chapter 7

The detective

At 4.15am on 20 January 2003, Detective Inspector Jonathan Morris's phone buzzes. He is on standby duty for the week, and he wakes on the first ring. After years of crime-scene calls, Morris is a light sleeper. A gust of wind can wake him.

Instructed to attend the crime scene immediately, he is given limited information about a mass murder that has taken place in Sea Point.

Forty-five minutes later, Morris joins a small group of his colleagues outside the house on Graham Road. The commotion and flashing lights have woken up the neighbourhood. Curious onlookers peer from the balconies of the surrounding blocks of flats.

The detective has a fleeting thought: these people have quite the view of the crime scene. He files the thought for later.

Violent crime is not uncommon in Sea Point, but this is something unique. Morris glances at the curious crowd gathering behind the crime-scene tape. It wouldn't be the first time a killer came back to the scene to watch the police work.

The most senior officer present is Captain Reynold Talmakkies. Morris greets Talmakkies and the two officers who flank him – Inspector Terrence Smart and Inspector Deon de Villiers. The men have worked many serious cases together. Talmakkies issues a briefing in rapid fire.

10 victims
4 barely clinging to life
6 dead
Bound
Gagged
Tortured
Cut
Shot

During the briefing, three officers from the Local Criminal Records Centre (LCRC) join the group. Captain Bruce Bartholomew handles forensic evidence – blood, hair, other DNA sources and fingerprints. Captain Arendse's ballistics skills are needed to understand the weapons that were used and the projectile trajectories. His expertise allows him to determine the type of crime committed solely by analysing the use of guns and bullets. Gang violence, robberies, personal murders and organised hits all have unique signatures, and Arendse has seen most of them in his time as a cop. The third LCRC member, Inspector Phillip Jacobs, has perhaps the most unenviable job on the team. While the others can focus on singular elements of the horror – a bullet, a bloodstain – Jacobs, as the videographer, takes it all in while his recorder films every inch of the scene – every victim and every injury without exception.

By the time Morris and his colleagues are ready to enter the scene at 5am, he already knows they are looking for two perpetrators. He sends up a silent prayer that the young man who dragged himself to the petrol station will survive. Morris's gut tells him Quinton Taylor will be a vital component of this case.

The scene that Morris encounters differs slightly from what Mark Hamilton and Captain Naude saw. Nick and his colleagues have, of course, already intervened to try to save lives. Paramedics will do their best not to interfere with the crime scene, but their priority is providing medical care to the victims, not preserving evidence. The remaining signs of their efforts to save the victims – a discarded section of a breathing tube, the plastic cover of a syringe – only add to the horror.

The paramedics would have first checked the victims' breathing. To do this, they had to remove the gags that the offenders had placed in their mouths. Wearing surgical gloves, they had pulled off the tape holding the socks in place and tossed them aside. It is Bartholomew's job to collect the tape and socks and preserve them for testing. Such items can be a significant source of fingerprints and DNA from the offender.

Morris, who has hunted serial killers, uncovered the graves of violated and murdered children, and collected scattered body parts from the scenes of ATM bombings, describes what he found at Graham Road as "the most gruesome scene I have ever experienced in my entire police career of 27 years".

At the entrance to the house, Jacobs switches on his video recorder to capture the scene. Besides the smell of petrol and blood that immediately hit him, one of Morris's most vivid memories will be the song playing on the television. It will become the unintended soundtrack to the crime-scene video, hauntingly playing in the background as the officers move through the house. Coincidentally, perhaps, it is also Morris's favourite song: Aaron Neville's 1966 hit *Tell It Like It Is*.

The first room Morris enters contains five of the victims. The paramedics had turned the men over, and they now lie on their backs next to each other. The detective notices that blood has soaked the carpet under the victims. The paramedics had also untied the white rope on the victims' hands and feet in places, or it had simply come loose in a struggle. It had clearly been too late for anyone to flee. Then, Morris's eye goes to the bullets and empty cartridges spread out across the carpet between the victims. Arendse will have his ballistics work cut out for him. He will eventually collect 11 bullets and casings – either 9mm or 7.65mm calibre – from this room alone

Behind the door, a wall safe stands open, the key still in the lock. A robbery? The smell of petrol bothers Morris, though. Who brings petrol to a robbery?

In the second room, he finds a victim lying on his side in a pool of blood. He's wearing denim jeans with a red shirt, and he was tied up and gagged like the other victims. A single bullet cartridge lies beside the body.

In the bathroom, Morris finds a pool of blood and two cartridges in front of the door. Someone explains that they transported this victim to the hospital. He moves through the rest of the house but finds little else of evidentiary value. Becoming overwhelmed by the smell of petrol and blood, he leaves the scene to the LCRC officers to process, reminding them to take regular breaks for fresh air.

Morris vividly recalls walking out of that scene feeling different. At most scenes, he would immediately snap into detective mode and focus on the next steps to take. This scene, though, made him pause for a moment before he could make that switch.

As he walks away from Graham Road towards his vehicle, he allows himself to consider the terror the victims must have experienced. What type of criminal is he hunting? Who could do something so savage? Morris has seen his fair share of monsters – those whom most people would describe as simply evil. He's seen behind their masks and had a peek at the sliver of humanity there. As he approaches his vehicle, he wonders whether there was even a shred of humanity in the men who had done this. Then, he unlocks his car and seals his emotions in a box so he can do his job. Feelings will do him no good right now. There are monsters to hunt.

Chapter 8

Eyewitnesses

Before Detective Inspector Morris arrived on the scene that morning, Captain Naude had already been looking for a car that was seen leaving Graham Road after gunshots were heard in the area, and he'd stumbled upon the scene at the Total garage by chance. There were several valuable but conflicting eyewitness accounts.

Morris has to interview these eyewitnesses and sort the important bits from the fluff. His first stop is Arthur's Seat Mansions, a block of flats in Arthurs Road, Sea Point, which forms a T-junction with Graham Road. The man he is there to see, Darren Brick, had been sitting in his parked car with his girlfriend, Robin Perl, on the corner of Marais Street and Graham Road at 3.15am that night, having a conversation after a night out. When they heard the faint sound of gunshots, they stopped talking and scanned the street, looking for suspicious activity. They spotted two men running down Graham Road. Brick says that the men were both wearing balaclavas, so he could not identify them, and they got into a white BMW and drove away. The couple then went to Sea Point police station to report the matter.

At 6.30am, Morris leaves Brick's home and returns to the scene. There, Director Riaan Booysen, the unit commander of the Serious and Violent Crimes Unit, officially appoints Morris as the lead investigator on the case.

Morris takes responsibility for securing the scene and remains at 7 Graham Road to oversee the evidence collection. The victims' bodies are transported to the Salt River mortuary. Morris gives instructions to his colleagues to carry out some of the less important parts of the investigation. He makes it clear, though, that no one but him is to talk to any of the survivors, should they be able to do so.

At 3pm, he locks up the house on Graham Road. He will keep the keys to the property for the rest of the investigation. Although he's been on the go for almost 12 hours, there is no time to rest. He has more eyewitnesses to interview.

Danie Theunissen is the first witness to give Morris an account of the perpetrators' appearance. It emerges that Theunissen had come close to death on the morning of 20 January 2003 after going to Sizzlers to see one of the workers. He tells Morris that he arrived at 1.20am and found the gate to the street open. He walked up the path and rang the buzzer at the front door. Soon, a coloured male opened the door. He tells Morris the man was between 35 and 40 years old, dressed neatly and in good shape, with short black hair.

Theunissen asked the man in Afrikaans if a specific worker he'd engaged with before was working that night.

The man kept the door partially closed and used his body to block the view into the house before responding, "No, there's nothing going on here tonight."

When Theunissen asked who else was on duty, the man barked, "I just told you, there is nothing going on here tonight!" He took the hint that his presence was unwanted and turned away.

Later in the day, he heard about the massacre and realised how close he'd come to being one of the victims. He called Sea Point police station, but the officer on duty was not being helpful. He then phoned a contact at the Triangle Project, an LGBTQ+ human rights organisation, who gave him the details of one of the officers on the scene.

Theunissen tells Morris that he will testify if necessary, and he is sure he will recognise the man again if he has to identify him.

There is no way that Theunissen could have known what was happening in the house that early morning. He did not hear screams or calls for help, and the man he spoke to, although rather abrupt in his manner, gave no indication he was dangerous. We now know that behind that half-closed door, 10 men were bound, gagged and being tortured.

All the Sizzlers victims were white males. There was a high probability that the man Theunissen had spoken to was one of the killers, as a client wouldn't have answered the door and sent another client away. The fact that the man did answer the door, though, brings another thought to Morris's mind. If this had been a robbery, why would the robbers have held the victims hostage for so long? Why would they have engaged with members of the public, sending them away to extend their time in the house? It made little sense.

Bordeaux Residential Apartments is an expansive complex occupying much of the block bordering Beach, Oliver, Marais and Graham roads in Sea Point. It has eight floors, and residents on the higher floors have an excellent view of the surrounding area from their balconies. This is where Morris heads next.

A witness, Jacobus Steyn, lives on the sixth floor of Bordeaux. He reported being woken at 3.20am on 20 January 2003 by the sound of gunshots. He grabbed his camera and went out onto his balcony. He saw two men holding guns running up Graham Road toward Marais Road. Steyn tells Morris that the individuals wore dark jackets and their faces were concealed with balaclavas. He then called the Sea Point police station to report what he had seen.

Morris also interviews Mark Hamilton and Captain Naude before finally calling it a day. As he prepares for bed, knowing that he'll replay the day's haunting images in his mind, he receives a phone call that reminds him the horror is far from over. The forensic pathologist will start the autopsies the next day at 8am, the caller says. Morris is instructed to attend.

Having an investigating officer attend the autopsy of a murder victim can be highly beneficial in solving cases. It gives the detective vital information about the victim and their cause of death. The officer can also provide details to the forensic pathologist that may be missing from the documentation accompanying the body.

This exchange of information has proved invaluable in several murder cases where the investigating officer attended the autopsy. Unfortunately, for reasons including a lack of resources, it happens rarely in South Africa, and victims of violent crime and their families are negatively affected. Perhaps as a result, many of South Africa's most successful police investigators (in terms of crime-solving rates) attend as many autopsies as their schedule allows. Morris is one of them.

The smells, sights and sounds of an autopsy are not pleasant. One can only imagine what the team attending the autopsies of the victims of the Sizzlers massacre experienced. Morris sits through them all, though. On both 21 and 22 January 2003, he stands by as Dr Lorna Martin and Dr Denise Lourens investigate and record the victims' gruesome and devastating injuries.

However, over the next few days, three of the surviving victims – Warren, Gregory and Marius – succumb to their injuries. Only one man, Quinton Taylor, has a positive prognosis, and even his condition is touch-and-go for some time.

Morris asks hospital staff to keep him updated on Quinton's condition. He wants to speak to him as soon as possible.

Chapter 9

The survivor

As Quinton Taylor collapsed on the concrete floor of the Total garage on the night of the massacre, he cried out, "Please help me. I don't want to die!" Bystanders tried to comfort the young man, and he was quickly taken to New Somerset Hospital in Green Point by ambulance.

Armed police officers kept watch over Quinton and the other survivors. At this point, the motive for the Sizzlers murders was unknown. If it had been an organised hit, it was possible the killers would come back to silence the survivors. No one was taking any chances. This also explains why the victims who survived, even briefly, were hard to find when their family members came looking for them. Police and hospital staff could not know for sure whether someone seeking one of the victims was a friend or a foe. So, if any phone calls were made to the hospital regarding these patients, it was likely the caller would be told they were not there.

As Quinton lay in the hospital bed, fighting for his

life, his identity was fiercely protected. He was given the pseudonym "Witness 74". Much later, once he was well enough to be discharged, he would be taken into the witness protection programme.

The maxillofacial surgeon who operated on Quinton to repair his shattered jaw would later testify that the young man was "lucky to be alive". Two bullets had been fired into his head. By a stroke of luck, grace or a combination thereof, both missed his brain. Even so, the swelling in his brain and the damage to his face could easily have been fatal. Thankfully, it wasn't.

Morris acknowledges that many theories were bandied about in those early days, but he ignored them all. He knew the key to solving the crime lay with the man who had lived through it. So, he ran down leads until Quinton could communicate with him. Then, on 26 January 2003, he got the call he'd been waiting for and rushed to Groote Schuur Hospital without delay.

Although Quinton was conscious, he still had stitches in his mouth from his operation, so he could not speak on the first day Morris met him. He introduced himself as the investigating officer but immediately realised that he would not get much out of Quinton. The young man looked tired and confused. Morris asked one question during that first interaction to confirm what the young man had originally said. How many attackers were there? Quinton raised his hand: two.

Morris visited Quinton in the hospital every day after that. Bit by bit, they put together a statement about the events of that night. There were many theories, suspicions and possibilities, but Quinton was the only person who knew the truth – and he had no reason to fabricate a story. He had survived what most people would consider their worst nightmare. This is the version of events that he gave Morris.

Quinton had only been working for Aubrey (whom he calls "Eric" in his statement) for about 10 days when the massacre occurred. He was living at the Sizzlers house on Graham Road with some of the other workers. He said that, to his knowledge, there were eight young men working for Aubrey at the time.

On 19 January 2003, he said, the occupants of the house had spent most of the day cleaning. Around 6pm, Aubrey said they could watch a movie. They chose *The Broken Hearts Club*. Quinton went outside a few times that night to smoke a joint, as they weren't allowed to smoke in the house.

While he was smoking his joint, a client (Gregory Berghaus) arrived and engaged Sergio de Castro in one of the studios.

Quinton's statement does not include the time of Gregory's arrival, whose name he did not know, but the sign-in roster found on the scene shows that the last client, who had to have been Berghaus despite having signed in as "Peter", arrived at 11.50pm.

Around midnight, Quinton smoked his last joint and went back inside, where a gangster movie was now playing.

Quinton and the other workers, except Sergio, were watching the movie in the room they shared, with bunk beds for all of them. He was lying on the top bunk, the other men were seated on chairs and Aubrey was in his own bedroom when the gate buzzer sounded. A few minutes later, Aubrey appeared in the bedroom doorway with two men Quinton hadn't seen before.

One man was a coloured male with short, curly, dark brown hair. The man was well built, with a prominent nose and a ruddy complexion. He was wearing a short-sleeved blue shirt, and Quinton estimated him to be in his late twenties to early thirties. The other man was a white male. He had straight black hair, brushed back. He was also wearing a short-sleeved blue shirt and had a fair complexion. Quinton describes this man as quite chubby, with a round stomach, and also in his late twenties to early thirties.

Aubrey motioned to the young men in the room and told the two new arrivals, "These are the masseurs I have available. You can choose which you would like to spend time with this evening." Quinton looked up as Aubrey said this, and the white male made eye contact with him.

"What are you doing?" the stranger asked.

"Just watching TV," Quinton responded.

Quinton's eyes moved to the men's hands, and he realised they were wearing surgical gloves. Within seconds, chaos erupted when the two men pulled firearms from their pants and pointed them around the room.

"We are going to rob you now, people," the white man said matter-of-factly.

In his statement, Quinton says both men addressed Aubrey as "Eric" (his industry name), and because they used his first name, Quinton got the distinct impression that they knew him.

The white male pointed his gun at Quinton and told him to get off the bunk bed and sit in a chair like the others. Both men then instructed the victims to remove and hand over all their jewellery. Everyone complied, placing their jewellery in a pile on the floor.

The white male asked Aubrey to open the safe behind the door in the room. Either Aubrey or Timothy unlocked the safe and then stepped back to sit down in their chairs.

The safe held the day's takings, which Quinton estimated could have been between R1,500 and R2,000. The sign-in roster found in Aubrey's room listed, among other information, the fee that a client had paid for services rendered. The sheet for Sunday 19 January 2003 showed takings of R840. However, two factors could have influenced this discrepancy. Quinton thought Aubrey usually banked each day's takings the next morning, but this would not have been possible on a Sunday. So, it's likely that the safe contained both Saturday and Sunday's takings, and perhaps even Friday's. It was also possible that the amount Aubrey had written on the roster was the fee due to the worker and not the total paid by the client. At this early stage of the investigation, it was interesting that the robbery (if that's what it was) had taken place at midnight on a Sunday, when the full weekend's takings would have been in the safe. This could have been a lucky guess on the part of the perpetrators or the result of inside information.

Besides the day's takings, Quinton had also given Aubrey R7,000 in cash for safekeeping, which was kept in a separate safe in Aubrey's room. Aubrey's brother-in-law, who knew where that safe was, would later tell police he'd found it open and empty.

The coloured male handed Timothy a roll of white nylon rope and instructed him to tie everyone up. Quinton had never seen the rope in the house, so he believed the men must have brought it with them. The initial instruction was for the men to be tied to their chairs, but it soon became apparent that Timothy, whether intentionally or not, was doing a poor job of binding the men. They could have easily escaped. The white male became enraged and snatched the rope from Timothy's hands. He told the victims to stand up and move the chairs back to the table they'd come from. The white male told the men to lie on their stomachs on the floor. Quinton recounts the men lay down in the following order: Timothy, Quinton, Aubrey, Johan, Marius, Travis, Stephanus and Warren at the far end.

Everyone complied with the instructions except Quinton. He told the men, "If I'm going to die, I want to see it coming."

Although there is no concrete medical proof, his refusal to lie face down could explain his survival and the differences between his wounds and those of the other victims. Even now, Quinton is strong-willed – someone who doesn't accept the status quo. It is probably something that's got him into trouble often, but on that night, it may have saved his life. In the years to come, the flickering flame inside him would carry him through dark times.

The white male gave the rope to the coloured male, who produced a knife from his pocket and cut it into lengths. He used these to hog-tie the men – wrists bound, ankles bound and tied together behind their backs. Quinton was tied up similarly, but his hands and feet were in front of him. The young man's eyes followed the men as they moved around the room. The coloured man said they would be gagged, and he opened cupboards to look for something suitable. He found several pairs of socks, placed one in each man's mouth and then stuck brown packing tape over them.

The doorbell rang a few times while the men were lying there.

We know that Danie Theunissen arrived at 1.20am and, according to his evidence, a coloured male came to the door and told him that there was "nothing going on here tonight". In his statement, though, Quinton mentions another visitor, one who was sent away by the white male. He told the visitor, "Sorry, folks, we are fully booked. Please come back tomorrow!" This means that there were other clients or visitors to Sizzlers that morning who did not come forward. It is possible they had not heard about the massacre or put the pieces together. They may have also thought their testimony would not be important. The most likely scenario is that the individuals who visited Sizzlers that night had been too afraid to come forward or did not want their identities linked to the case for fear of recrimination.

Lying on his back in the bedroom, Quinton had no concept of time. Shortly after the men had been tied up, the white male called the coloured male into the kitchen. They talked for a bit and then returned to the bedroom. Quinton saw the white male was now armed with a knife. He recognised it as one of Aubrey's steak knives from the kitchen.

Keep in mind that during this time, Sergio de Castro and Gregory Berghaus were still engaged in their appointment in Studio 1. The two men in the house did not know they were there. Gregory had arrived at 11.50pm. According to the roster sheet, clients ordinarily spent at least one hour at an appointment, but this was a fluid arrangement: if the time was extended, they'd simply pay an additional amount before they left. If we use Theunissen's time of arrival at the house as a marker, this means that the men had already been in the house for at least an hour and a half at this point. Sergio and Gregory could have emerged from Studio 1 at any moment.

Quinton recalls how the men moved around the house for some time and realised some rooms were locked. The studios at Sizzlers were only unlocked for cleaning and to allow clients to enter and exit. They were kept locked at all other times to minimise the possibility of theft. While the young men were on duty, they did not have access to their cellphones, as Aubrey didn't want them to be distracted. So, all the phones were locked away in whichever studio was the least likely to be used that night.

The white male entered the bedroom and ripped the tape off Aubrey's mouth. He demanded the keys to Studio 3. Aubrey said he didn't know where they were and looked over at Johan, who had been the last to have the keys. The tape was ripped off his mouth, too. Johan said he did not know where the keys were. He told the man that there was nothing of value in Studio 3 anyway, only some luggage and empty bags. The man searched Johan and found the keys in his pocket. He gagged both Aubrey and Johan again and left the room.

Minutes later, he returned with several cellphones in his hands. He shouted at Johan, demanding to know why he had lied. The man's anger erupted into rage and, within seconds, he and his cohort were looming over the men, knives in hand.

The sound of his coworkers' screams filled Quinton's ears as the attackers stabbed and slashed at them. The coloured male appeared over Quinton and sliced his neck.

Out of the corner of his eye, Quinton saw Aubrey had loosened the rope that bound him. Soon, he was up on his knees, wrestling with the two armed men. The men attacked Aubrey with their knives, and he fell backwards. This explains Aubrey's distinct injuries, including the bite mark, that were noted in his autopsy.

The white male left the room after this and returned with a two-litre bottle of petrol. He poured the petrol over the men. Aubrey screamed through his gag, begging the men not to burn them and to just take what they want and leave. Once the petrol bottle was empty, the men left the room and Quinton heard the hum of their voices in the passage. He could not make out most of their conversation but heard the last sentence. The white male instructed the other man to go back into the bedroom and watch over the victims. The white male then walked around the house, opening cupboards and rummaging around for a while. Occasionally, the pair met up in the passageway and smoked cigarettes together. Quinton got the feeling that they were not in a hurry and briefly wondered how long they had been there and how much longer they planned to stay.

When the coloured man was alone with them in the room, the victims who could still speak asked if he was going to kill them. "No," he said. Quinton described this man as seemingly "decent" while the other was "weird and aggressive". It seems the other victims also got the impression that this perpetrator was perhaps more reasonable than the other.

Several smoke breaks later, Quinton says, the white male grew increasingly angry. He paced up and down the hallway, swearing and muttering under his breath. The coloured man tried to placate him, asking him to calm down in both English and Afrikaans.

Remember that Quinton Taylor's statement only contains

what he saw and heard during the crime. There are, of course, missing pieces, including how Sergio and Gregory were attacked, which Quinton would not have seen and could not testify to. (These details would be uncovered later by other evidence.)

Despite the coloured male's best efforts to calm his accomplice, the white male's anger erupted again. Suddenly, he flicked his half-smoked cigarette out the window and stomped towards Studio 1. Quinton heard four gunshots. The coloured male was visibly shocked at the sound of gunfire and pulled his own gun out of his pants as if he thought he was at risk.

Without warning, the white male walked back into the bedroom – and both men started firing at the victims. Quinton lost consciousness at some point, but his subconscious absorbed the sounds of countless gunshots going off around him. This would form part of his memories later. When he came to, he managed to untie himself. He looked around at his coworkers. Everyone was lying very still. In a daze, he called out and asked if everyone was okay. No one answered. Unaware of the extent of his injuries but fuelled by adrenaline, he stumbled through the house. In Studio 1, he found Sergio lying on the floor. There was no response from him either. In the bathroom, Quinton found the client lying on his back. Passing by Aubrey's room, he saw all the cupboards were open and items were scattered about.

He slowly made his way to the Total garage, leaving the door open behind him. A trail of blood would later bear testament to the young man's journey that night. In a sliding-doors moment, just as Quinton disappeared around the corner, Mark Hamilton's taxi pulled up to the kerb.

Chapter 10

The net closes

Detective Inspector Jonathan Morris's initial instinct is to ignore the wild theories being touted in the media. There are whispers of the massacre being an organised-crime hit carried out by street gangs or drug dealers. Others say it's a targeted hate crime.

Years later, Morris laughs darkly as he remembers one instance where an officer attached to the Occult Crimes Unit decided to visit the scene. Upon finding a bucket of bloodied water in the corner of the room, the officer announced it was a clear indication of ritualistic behaviour from the killers. Morris raised an eyebrow and informed the man that this was the bucket the ballistics officer had used to wash the bullets he'd collected. That put paid to one theory at least.

Morris remains single-minded in his focus. His attention is on the lone survivor, and on 4 February 2003 it pays off.

As he painstakingly takes Quinton's statement from his hospital bed, his colleagues at Sea Point police station are gathering photo albums of previously arrested persons. Criminals often work in the same geographical areas repeatedly. These are usually areas where they have some level of comfort: they may live there, work there or know the area in another context. Police keep mugshots of arrested suspects to help eyewitnesses identify criminals. To avoid unfair bias, the photographs are not accompanied by names. Each photograph bears a reference number, and there is a separate index book that only police officers can access. This book links the names of suspects to their photographs.

The photo albums also do not contain any information about the crime for which the suspect was arrested. Again, this is to avoid even unintentional bias. Criminals' actions tend to escalate. Even if a suspect was previously arrested for assault, they may also be sought in a murder. Many arrests are linked to minor crimes not even related to a major crime being investigated. Ted Bundy, a well-known American serial killer, was apprehended for a traffic offence. South African serial killers are often caught for rape when a victim escapes, and then their DNA is linked to multiple murders. In the Sizzlers case, a car that wasn't returned on time snared a mass murderer.

Inspector Deon de Villiers receives three photo albums from the senior administrative clerk at Sea Point police station on 4 February 2003. He drives directly to Groote Schuur Hospital where, by now, the nurses are used to seeing the heavily armed guards outside Quinton Taylor's room. They always look the other way when Morris or one of his colleagues have to speak to the young man outside visiting hours. Many of the same nurses tried, in vain, to save the lives of Warren, Marius and Gregory.

They want the men who had done such horrific things to be caught, too. So, as long as Quinton is strong enough, they allow the officers to come and go as needed.

De Villiers settles into a chair beside Quinton Taylor's hospital bed. He explains that he will hand him some photo albums. The men who killed his colleagues and attacked him may or may not be in the albums.

"Take your time and look carefully. If you see the men, or either of them, point to their photograph."

Quinton nods. His mouth is still incredibly tender, and he struggles to speak. He's tired, but he knows this is important and he'll give it his best shot. The men's faces are seared into his memory. He knows that if they are in these three albums, he will recognise them immediately.

And he does.

Midway through the second album, Quinton's heart rate accelerates. The monitor beeps angrily. His eyes bore into the album. He raises a shaking hand and thrusts his forefinger onto the page. De Villiers stands up and looks where he's pointing: 2899. He checks to see if his voice recorder is still running.

"Quinton, I need you to say the number of the photograph you are pointing to in the book out loud for me, please."

Quinton swallows. "2 ... 8 ... 9 ... 9 ..."

It's hard to say the numbers with his contorted mouth, but he continues. "His hair," he says, gesturing to his own head where his hair was cut by the surgeons who saved his life, "it's longer there, but this is the coloured guy."

De Villiers fills out the required paperwork and waits while Quinton goes through the rest of the albums. He doesn't find the other man, but the officer is unperturbed. One is enough for now. He thanks Quinton and tells him to rest, reassuring him that he or Morris will update him as soon as they have made an arrest.

In the days that follow, Quinton Taylor is discharged from the hospital. He is still known only as Witness 74. Morris and the young man have one last meeting to resolve any remaining matters before he is whisked away by the Witness Protection Unit to an unknown location where he will stay until police feel it is safe for him to return home. He leaves the house only for medical care and, even then, it is under heavily armed guard. The hospital visits are swift and organised with military precision.

From Groote Schuur, De Villiers goes directly back to Sea Point police station. When the administrative clerk sees him, she can tell from his expression that more work awaits – and it's good news. She pulls out the index book that will match the number on the photograph to a name. De Villiers shows her the completed identification form and the number: 2899. Her finger runs down the list to the number and the name beside it: Trevor Theys.

Theys had been added to the police photo album in 1990. He was 13 years younger in the photograph Quinton pointed out, but De Villiers had seen how certain he was. More than a decade before, Theys had taken a friend's vehicle and not returned it on time. The owner reported his vehicle as being used without his consent, and Trevor was arrested. De Villiers contacts Morris and hands over his findings. Morris takes the baton and runs with it.

Individual South African Police Service (SAPS) branches are only involved in investigations until the suspect is arrested. They do not keep records of the outcome of trials. This is the mandate of the Local Criminal Record Centres (LCRCs), of which there are 92 across the country. The nearest LCRC is Morris's next destination.

The LCRC officers make quick work of fleshing out Trevor Theys's background. In 1991, he was found guilty and given a choice between a fine of R500 or 100 days in prison for the case in Sea Point in which he was arrested. In addition, he was given a suspended sentence of 200 days' imprisonment, which would become effective if he committed any robbery, theft or housebreaking offences within a three-year period. He was also ordered to pay R100 in compensation to the victim.

The LCRC officer also has a firearm licence on record for Theys. Morris's lips twitch into a smile at the sight of the calibre. In 1995, Theys was licensed to own a CZ 7.65 pistol. The bullets on the scene at Sizzlers were 9mm and 7.65mm.

The last piece of information provides a starting point to find the man who could be responsible for the murders of nine men and the attempted murder of one: his registered address – 48 Hector Road, Grassy Park. Morris thanks the LCRC officers and grabs his car keys. His destination is Grassy Park.

Chapter 11

Trevor Theys

Eyewitness Darren Brick reported seeing a white BMW fleeing the scene on the night of the murders. Detective Inspector Morris wants to see whether Trevor Theys owns such a vehicle, but the eNatis system, which contains the details of vehicles registered to South African drivers, comes up blank. Of course, that doesn't mean that Theys is not driving a white BMW – just that he hasn't registered it in his name.

From 6pm on 4 February 2003, Morris holds surveillance in Hector Street, looking out for a white BMW arriving home. He sees nothing of interest that night.

He could have easily walked up to 48 Hector Street, knocked on the door and asked to speak with Theys to feel him out and see if he had an alibi for the night of the murders. Morris knows better, though. Theys, like many other criminals, will run at the first sign of the police. In the days after a crime, offenders lie low. They're often jumpy and paranoid. It would take very little for his suspect to flee the province, and then they might never track him down again.

So, just as he had so patiently waited for Quinton Taylor to regain consciousness and give him the information he needed, Morris now draws on his patience again.

He submits the J50 paperwork required to apply for an arrest warrant to the Cape Town Magistrate's Court. Within days, he gets the news that the warrant has been approved.

On 12 February 2003, Morris parks his vehicle a few blocks away from Hector Street and walks to number 48. He walks as though he is simply taking a stroll through the neighbourhood. As he passes the house, he makes a note of the layout, the exit points and any risky areas Theys could use to his advantage. He calculates how many police officers they'll need to conduct the arrest safely and where they should be positioned. Like a lion stalking an antelope, he does not intend pouncing too soon. Everything needs to be in place first. With his initial surveillance done, Morris contacts a crack team of police officers. These are colleagues he trusts implicitly and whose experience matches or exceeds his own. As the investigating officer, he will take the lead in Theys's arrest, and he wants only the best as backup.

At 5am on 13 February 2003, four men gather in the parking area of Ottery Hypermarket. Morris is joined by Superintendent Mike Barkhuizen, Detective Inspector Okkert Brits and Detective Sergeant Kenneth Speed. Between them, the officers have tracked and arrested hundreds of high-profile offenders across the country. They regularly appear in court to testify to the roles they played in solving heinous crimes, and this is when their names appear in news articles. Mostly, they work behind the scenes. No one, least of all the suspects, knows they are on the trail until handcuffs click around wrists. That's the way they like it. Moving under the radar is necessary, essential even, when you're looking for people who don't want to be found. Today, they plan to find Trevor Theys.

As exciting as a breaking-dawn raid seems, disappointment arises – as is often the case with police work – when the four officers descend on the house in Hector Street. Just like details of cars, registered addresses are a lucky draw. Sometimes people don't update their information when they move. Theys no longer lives at the house, the rather surprised tenant tells the four heavily armed police officers surrounding him. He knows where Theys's ex-wife moved to, though.

Theys and his wife, Janap, had lived at 48 Hector Street until recently when their fiery relationship imploded and they separated. The minute Morris and the other officers hear the word "ex", their eyes meet and they exchange knowing smiles. They've struck gold.

The only thing better than finding your suspect where you thought he would be is finding your suspect's ex-partner first. Exes often have axes to grind, regardless of gender, and they know things your suspect doesn't want you to know.

Janap Theys had moved just a six-minute drive from Hector Street. Morris and his colleagues pull up in front of her house and knock on the door. Morris takes just one of his colleagues with him. The other two wait within shouting distance. They don't believe Trevor is in the house, and they don't want to scare Janap. But the woman is unfazed by the police officers in her home. She is friendly and chatty. Morris says that he is looking for Trevor and asks whether she knows his address.

"It's for speeding fines again, isn't it?" Janap exclaims. Morris stays silent. He doesn't agree or disagree; he just smiles. She can interpret that however she pleases. Janap takes his silence as agreement and continues, "He's always getting my brother in trouble with speeding fines. Every time he uses his BMW."

Morris nods. "Your brother owns a BMW?"

"Yes," Janap says, "a white one. Trevor uses it a lot. Sometimes without my brother's permission, but I think he's going to stop letting Trevor use it now if you catch him for these fines."

The likelihood that Trevor will ever drive that BMW again is very low.

Janap gives Morris two house numbers in Sonderend Street, Mitchells Plain. She says the homes belong to Trevor's brother and sister who live across the road from each other. "Don't trust them, sir, because they can lie a lot," she warns Morris in Afrikaans. "If he isn't at his brother Andrew's house, then he is over the road at his sister's house. Please catch him and arrest him because he also hasn't paid maintenance money for a long time!"

Morris thanks Janap and promises her he will arrest Trevor. He doesn't tell her that it won't be for traffic offences or outstanding maintenance.

At 7.15am, the four officers arrive at Trevor's brother's house. Morris goes up to the door while the other three officers spread out on the street, watching both Andrew Theys's and his sister's houses. Morris knocks, and a man at the door introduces himself as Andrew Theys, confirming his identity. Andrew says that Trevor is not there, and he doesn't know where he is. As Morris walks back down the pathway to the street, Brits informs him he has just seen movement in a window at the house across the road. Someone peeked around the curtain and then drew it shut.

The men cross the road. This time, they all approach the house. Morris stands at the door, with the others out of sight around the side of the house. He knocks and a coloured male with short brown hair opens the door. He immediately recognises him from his mugshot.

"Are you Trevor Theys?" Although Theys immediately admits his identity, his body gives him away as well. Morris can see the man's heart thumping through his tight white shirt. He begins to breathe heavily as well.

Morris advises his suspect of his rights and informs him he is under arrest on nine murder charges and one charge of attempted murder. Theys shows no signs of surprise as Morris rattles off the long list of charges.

"Where is your firearm?" Morris asks.

"I don't have it anymore," Theys claims. "I gave some guys a lift, and they robbed me."

"Did you report it stolen?" Theys shakes his head in response, his mouth a tight line.

Morris has an arrest warrant but not a search warrant for Trevor's sister's house. After confirming that one bedroom in the house is his current place of residence, Morris asks Trevor for his permission to search the room. Trevor agrees.

Barkhuizen conducts the search while Morris takes Trevor across the road to Andrew's house. The officer informs the man that Trevor has been arrested in connection with several murders. Andrew steps aside and allows the officers and his brother into the home. Brits leads Trevor into the kitchen, and Morris hangs back with Andrew.

"The murders were committed with 9mm and 7.65mm weapons. Your brother claims his 7.65 was stolen. You don't know anything about a 9mm, maybe?" Morris asks.

A shadow moves over Andrew's face, and his eyes flick to his brother seated and handcuffed in the kitchen. "Can we talk outside?"

Andrew Theys shifts his weight between his feet as he stands next to Morris in his front garden. He pulls the front door closed.

"Last month, my 9mm went missing from my safe. I believe Trevor stole it. He said it wasn't him. I reported it to the police." Andrew's voice is low. He doesn't want to be in this position, but he also does not want his firearm linked to a mass murder. Later, Morris will find the report Andrew filed about his missing firearm, which proves his story.

Andrew Theys stands at the front door of his home, watching his brother being led away by the four police officers. At various times over the past few years, nine other men also walked out of their family homes for the last time. Andrew at least has the small privilege of understanding that he will probably never see his brother outside prison again. The victims' family members did not know that when *they* said goodbye, it would be the last time.

Chapter 12

The interview

Trevor Theys is booked into the police holding cells while Morris takes his time to strategise before questioning the suspect. Although he wants a full confession, Morris's tactics are different from the heavy-handed nature of some police officers. Throughout his career, creating connections with suspects to get them to talk has served him well. Many of the suspects who have confessed to him saw him almost as a father figure.

Morris is to the point but not abrasive or aggressive. Above all, he wants the suspects he's questioning to know that he sees their humanity despite their horrific crimes. Often, by the time some criminals find themselves sitting in front of Morris, they barely see themselves as human beings. The warmth of Morris's demeanour seldom fails to touch even the most damaged souls.

Around 9.15am, Morris brings Theys in for his interview. Morris is relaxed and offers Trevor coffee, which he readily accepts. When he asks to smoke, Morris says it's no problem. He's not indulging the man unnecessarily, but if Theys is comfortable, he's more likely to talk. A smoker thinking of nothing but a nicotine hit is a recipe for a stilted interview.

Theys drags on his cigarette. Billows of smoke fill the interview room. Morris gets ready to pose his first question, but Theys beats him to it. "What evidence do you have against me?"

Morris pulls out the mugshot photo that Quinton Taylor identified and pushes it toward Theys.

"You've aged well," Morris quips. "The witness who identified you from this photo knew it was you right away."

Theys eyes the photograph, more than likely remembering the night it was taken and inwardly cursing at how such a minor transgression could have landed him in this situation.

"Is that all?" Theys asks hopefully.

"You are also the owner of a CZ 7.65 pistol." Morris doesn't really believe the story about it being stolen. "The same calibre cartridges were found on the scene. Those bullets were also found in the bodies of the victims."

Theys doesn't ask Morris for more information, but he offers it anyway. "I have a witness who saw two men leaving the crime scene in a white BMW. Your brother-in-law owns a white BMW, which I know you have driven in the past."

Morris tries to maintain eye contact with Theys, but the man's gaze drops to the floor. "Yes," he says after a long moment of silence. "I was involved."

Morris nods. He remains a picture of calm, but inside he's bursting. Theys tells him he has a heart condition and asks if he can arrange for his medication to be brought to him.

"Of course," Morris says readily. "I'll fetch it from your family myself."

Theys stands up and shakes Morris's hand, and then, quite unexpectedly (although he's not the first suspect to do so with the detective), pulls him in for a hug.

"My life is in your hands now," Theys says. "You're the only person who can help me."

"I will do whatever I can to help you, Trevor," Morris says, "but you've got to tell me who the other guy is and where he lives. Are you prepared to give your confession to a magistrate?"

Theys is nodding already. "Yes, yes," he says, almost eagerly. "I'll tell you about Adam and take you to his flat."

Adam.

It's the first time Morris hears the name that will haunt him for the rest of his career: Adam Woest. He just wants to pile Trevor into his vehicle and go to Woest's apartment, but as he has done throughout the investigation, he remains in careful predator mode. Each step must be methodically planned. Failure to do so could cause two mass murderers to walk free. So, before Trevor Theys goes anywhere, he must be taken to a magistrate to make a full confession.

In South Africa, a confession given to the investigating officer during an interview is not admissible as evidence. The officer can listen if the suspect wants to talk, but if he changes his mind later, there's little evidentiary value to the conversation. To be accepted by a court, a confession must be made in the presence of a magistrate who ensures no coercion has taken place and that there's full awareness of rights.

False confessions, even to crimes as heinous as mass

murder, are not uncommon. People will do strange things to get out of the pressurised environment of an interview room, which is one of the reasons for this safeguard. It protects everyone involved, but it makes the investigating officer's job more difficult. Striking while the iron is hot is imperative. If a magistrate can't be located immediately, the delay could lead to the suspect changing their mind about confessing or deciding they'd prefer to speak to a lawyer first. Thankfully for Morris, considering he started his day so early, it is relatively easy to find a magistrate to take the confession.

By noon, Trevor Theys is standing in the chambers of the Cape Town Magistrate's Court. To avoid accusations of undue influence, Morris temporarily transfers custody of Theys to an officer not involved in the case to carry out this part of the process.

Chapter 13

The first confession

At 1.07pm, Trevor Theys relays his confession to Magistrate Alida le Roux. The following is a transcript of that confession:

Last year, I think it was during the winter, I used to frequent Walter's Pub and Grill [just known as Walter's Grill] *at Sea Point, where I befriended most of the staff. One evening, the manager named Adam* [Woest] *told me* [that] *one of the boys who worked at Sizzlers* [had] *told him that a substantial amount of cash was kept on the premises. He said that it was easy to rob them.*

I was actually joking when I said we can do it. He spoke of finding guns and said because I am a coloured, that in the township it would be easy for me to find weapons. I just played along and when he asked me how far I got, my reply was nothing yet.

I had a girlfriend who is 20 years old, but she broke my heart with another woman. I tried to get her back but could not. Then one evening when no one was at home,

I took my brother's gun and my own gun and phoned Adam and told him that I found the guns so we can do it the same night.

He phoned Sizzlers and told them that he was a client. We entered the premises; the manager let us in.

The manager took us to a room and [Adam] told the manager that he preferred blond boys. When the boy came, Adam took out my brother's gun. I gave Adam the gun before the time.

Adam told the boy to take us to the rest of the boys. One of the boys called the owner and said it was a robbery. They gave us the cash that was in the two safes. It was less than R2,000. I thought it was not worth taking it. Adam put the money in his pocket.

He made them to lie down and tied them up with their hands behind their backs and also tied their feet so that when we leave, they could not switch on the alarm, but Adam didn't want to leave.

He then gave me a knife and told me to slit their throats, which I did not want to do. I told him to do it. He then said to me that well, we both must do it. He started at one end and I started at the other end.

In the act, I could not do it as I didn't know how. I really did not want to do it. But Adam was a bigger man than me. I was fighting for my own life because Adam said that he will get rid of loose ends.

When I slit their throats, I only gave them flesh wounds. I slit four of them. It was not deep cuts. They would not die from these wounds. I know that.

Adam slit the throats of, I think, four of them from the one side. They were all in the same room. I then went and drank some water. Adam was still with them. They started screaming – the boys whose throats were slit.

When I returned to the room where the boys were, the next-door room door opened. There were two men, one man and one boy, in that room. We made them to lie down and tied them in the same manner as the others. Adam stayed with them, and I stayed in the room with the rest of the boys.

I was talking to them, calming them. They asked me whether they were going to die. I promised them that no one will die. Later, me and the boys spoke to each other. We were actually laughing and joking. They were calming me, and I was calming them.

Adam was waiting. I don't know for what. He kept on showing me the guns; that we must use the guns. I refused. Half the time I didn't know what I was doing because my girlfriend hurt me.

I was still speaking to the boys. I turned around and Adam was not there. I walked up into the hallway. I went to check the other two who were in the next room. One of the men was free and coming out of the room. There was a gun on the table in the hallway. I picked it up and told him to go back. The man ran down the hallway to the kitchen. I followed.

Adam was in the kitchen looking for something and the man attacked him, then he turned around and attacked me. I didn't know what I was doing. I first hit him with the gun on his head. The man attacked me on my face, choking me or something. The firearm went off, and the man fell down. I just stood there.

Adam took the gun from me and went to the first room

where the boy was left still tied up. He shot the boy. I walked in front of Adam. Adam stood in the doorway when he shot the boy. The boy was not facing Adam, but was with his back to Adam. Adam was close to the boy when he shot the boy. I was standing next to Adam when he shot the boy. Then Adam told me that now it was too late, that we have to shoot them.

The reason I think, is because Adam lives in Sea Point and I worked in Sea Point. The boys may recognise us.

He told me to go from one side and shoot them, whilst he went from the other side. I felt compelled because I was scared and fearing for my own life. I am not that kind of person. I was scared to die.

Adam started shooting first. All the boys were tied up with hands and feet, lying on their stomachs. I also shot. I shot four boys at the back of their heads. The boys were still alive. Adam then gave me the keys to the safety gate. I struggled to open it, but eventually I did.

There is something I forgot Adam brought with to rob. He had it on him. Duct tape, gloves and masks. Two pairs of gloves and two pairs of masks. The boys were also gagged.

Then he put on the mask. I did too. We got out of the house and ran to the car. We started the car and drove down to Beach Road. We went down Beach Road on the freeway past the Waterfront.

When we got to Paarden [Eiland], we threw out the masks and gloves. We had the gloves on since we arrived. We then drove to Bellville. We then stayed until sunlight. On Voortrekker Road, Bellville, Adam told me that he was going home and will take a taxi back to Sea Point. I continued to drive. I drove a white BMW – the same car

93

we used to get away. I went on the N1, not the N2, it's the N1. I just wanted to get away. I feared what might happen. I went to Paarl, bought me other clothes, then continued to drive on the N1. I still had the other clothes I wore. On the pass I changed clothes and kept the other clothes in the bag.

I went through the tunnel, past Worcester, towards Beaufort West. I then discovered that I had both guns in the car. I dismantled it. Whilst I was driving, I threw it out of the window piece by piece along the roadside. I don't know how far I travelled on the N1. Before I got to Beaufort West, I turned back and returned to Cape Town.

I didn't know where to go and what to do. I drove around night and day, only going home to wash and change for two days. I then decided to go home. I stayed there. I didn't work. Instead, I repaired my mother's car and sister's car.

One night in Cape Town, the owner of the BMW came to fetch his car, Mr Stephens, but he doesn't know anything about this. I rented the vehicle from him.

I just stayed at home for about three weeks. I decided to work again. I then phoned Adam to borrow petrol money to start working, because I transport ladies to and from work – escort agencies and to hotels and clients. I started on Monday 10 February 2003.

This morning I was across the road from where I live at my sister's, drinking coffee and playing solitaire. A knock came to the door.

Everybody else in the house was sleeping. I saw men running around the side of the house. I knew they were coming for me. They were police. I opened the door. The officer asked me my name. I told them.

Since that time, I have been cooperating with them fully, because I am sorry about what happened. They took me to my room asking for my firearm licence. Then they told me why. They informed me about my rights. They said I had the right to an attorney and if I cannot afford a lawyer, a legal aid attorney will be supplied to me free of charge. They also told me that I have the right to remain silent and that I didn't need to incriminate myself in any way. I was then arrested for the murders at Sizzlers. I then fully cooperated. I told them I will show them where I threw away the guns out of the car.

That is all.

After completing his confession, Trevor Theys goes with Morris and Barkhuizen to point out Adam Woest's place of residence. The apartment block is familiar to Morris. He also visited it on the day of the murders to interview Jacobus Steyn, the eyewitness who lived there. Theys shows the detectives the apartment where Woest lives. He tells the officers that he lives there with his girlfriend, Adele.

It's 2.20pm at this point. Theys says that Woest is already likely to be on shift at his restaurant job, but Adele works ordinary office hours and will be home shortly.

Barkhuizen elects to remain behind to talk to Woest's girlfriend. Morris leaves with Theys and they head off to the district surgeon. At 3.15pm, Theys is examined for injuries while his hair and blood samples are collected.

This check-up serves a dual purpose. The first is directly

related to the investigation. Although it has been some time since the crime occurred, any injuries on Theys's body may be relevant to the case. The second purpose is to protect the police from claims of misconduct relating to assault. It is not uncommon for offenders – especially those who have confessed – to claim they were assaulted by police and have their confessions thrown out of court. Theys is about to be booked into the awaiting-trial section of a prison. Although the Department of Correctional Services has a mandate to protect suspects and offenders, the prison environment is volatile, and fights break out regularly. Any injuries Theys has when going in must be recorded to safeguard everyone involved. Morris has to play this one by the book. He is far too close to cracking the case wide open.

Chapter 14

Woest

Adele van den Heever arrives home on 13 February 2003 to find a man she doesn't recognise standing next to her apartment door. Superintendent Barkhuizen introduces himself. He is careful about what he says because, at this point, he doesn't know for sure that Adele will not cover for Adam Woest in some way. While an ex-partner can be extremely beneficial to investigators, as was the case with Janap Theys, a current partner can be equally damaging.

Barkhuizen shows Adele his identification and asks if he can speak to her about a case he is investigating. She is hesitant and a little taken aback, but she agrees and opens the apartment door. Inside, Adele confirms she lives with Adam Woest and that they are in a relationship. Slowly, Barkhuizen eases Adele into the conversation. He wants to get as much information out of her as possible before he reveals her boyfriend is a suspect in a mass murder. If she is as clueless about his involvement as she seems, that information will probably shut her down completely and she'll be of no use from that point.

First, he ascertains her whereabouts on the evening of 19 January 2003. It turns out Adele wasn't even in the Western Cape. She left Sea Point on 18 January 2003 to spend some time with her family in Boksburg and Potchefstroom. She tells Barkhuizen that she returned on 31 January 2003. As she was not there on the night of the massacre, she cannot verify Adam's whereabouts.

Then Barkhuizen asks whether Adele had heard about the massacre at Sizzlers. Of course, she says, she and Adam had even known some of the young men and the owner of the establishment. As the police officer carefully begins to lay out why he is sitting in her apartment, he sees something change in her expression. He hasn't even said the words yet, but her hand is already covering her mouth as if she is preparing to stifle a scream of horror.

By the time Barkhuizen says the words, Adele is shaking her head and trembling. Chewing her lip, she tells him that when she got home from her holiday, Adam was acting strangely. He had changed his hair and was constantly wearing his spectacles, which she'd previously had to force him to wear at least when he was reading.

"He's not a very outgoing guy in general, but with me, he is usually talkative," she says. "But the last few days he's been very quiet. I asked him what was wrong, but he wouldn't say."

Adele says that Adam appeared jumpy and nervous whenever they saw police officers on the street or when a police van drove past.

She had never known him to be interested in the news, but after she returned home, he bought the paper every day, devouring any information about the Sizzlers massacre. She also heard him saying to his friend Trevor Theys that there hadn't been any proper media coverage of the crime until three days after it happened. Adele had put this interest down to the fact that Adam had known some of the victims. She had found it traumatic too. Now, though, she realises his interest in the case may have been for very different reasons.

Barkhuizen carefully selects a crime-scene photograph that is not particularly graphic but clearly shows the white nylon rope the victims were bound with. He shows it to Adele. In Theys's confession, he claimed that Woest had supplied the rope and tape they'd used to bind the victims.

"Have you ever seen rope like this before?" Barkhuizen asks. Adele sucks in a breath and nods. Tears are streaming from her eyes.

She had kept a roll of white nylon rope, just like that, in her bathroom. After she returned from Gauteng, she noticed it was gone and asked Adam whether he'd moved it or used it for something. He told her he did not know what she was talking about.

Adele van den Heever's life changes that afternoon. She is thrust into the middle of an investigation into a horrific mass murder, and the man she thought she loved is accused of orchestrating it.

Barkhuizen asks Adele for a picture of Adam. He explains that they will take him into custody and, for her own safety, she should not contact him. If she tries to alert Adam to his imminent arrest, she could put lives in jeopardy. Adele nods. She understands. At that moment, she isn't sure she ever wants to speak to Adam again anyway.

At 6pm, Morris collects the photograph of Adam Woest from Barkhuizen. He has now been on duty for more than 12 hours, but his day is not even close to finished. He'll sleep after he handcuffs Woest.

Initially, the plan is that members of the Crime Intelligence Unit will carry out the arrest. Members of this unit are skilled in surveillance and intercepting suspects with the least amount of fuss and risk to the public. Morris agrees to remain on standby at the SAPS office in Sea Point, but becomes frustrated after hours of waiting. He telephones Detective Sergeant Speed and asks him to accompany him to Quay Four restaurant at the V&A Waterfront, where Woest works.

Morris and Speed sit outside the restaurant in their vehicle for half an hour, waiting to see if they can spot Woest, before they decide to go inside. Morris introduces himself to the manager and asks if he can speak to her in private. She agrees and leads the officers through the back-of-house section of the restaurant to her office. The corridor takes them past the kitchen, where Morris sees Woest. A kitchen is not the safest of places to arrest a suspect who is believed to have committed nine violent murders. He does not want to get into a confrontation that could end badly, so he says nothing and follows the manager to her office.

He briefs the woman, giving her only vague information but enough for her to understand that the situation is serious and that her compliance is required. She nods and picks up the phone to dial the extension in the kitchen.

Her voice quivers a little as someone picks up and she asks, "Please have Adam come to my office."

The officers stand and flank the door. Less than a minute later, a knock sounds and in walks Adam Woest. Speed closes the door behind him, while Morris steps out in front of Woest. As Morris places his hand on Woest's arm, the man's head swivels between the detectives and his boss. Morris introduces himself and Speed and immediately states Woest's rights and the charges on which he is being detained. As the officers cuff Woest, he says nothing. His boss's face turns a sickly shade of pale as she hears the words, "nine counts of murder, one count of attempted murder".

Morris transports Woest to the Sea Point police station. He takes him into the interview room and, just as in Theys's interview, Woest speaks first.

"How did you know about me?" An admission of sorts. Morris responds with two words that reveal to Woest the extent of his exposure.

"Trevor Theys." Woest visibly deflates. "I know you supplied the rope, the gloves and the balaclavas, and Trevor supplied the firearms and the car."

Morris gazes evenly into Woest's eyes, which he describes as cold and dark. He lets his words sink in and then delivers what he calls "the killer blow".

"Trevor Theys has already given a full confession to a magistrate," Morris says. Woest's mouth hangs open slightly. "He's implicated you as the mastermind."

Woest starts to shake his head. "Well, you'd better get me

a magistrate too because I also want to put my confession on record."

Morris can't believe his luck. Two confessions in one day. Both mass murderers in cuffs. He doesn't give Woest time to change his mind and makes the call to Serious and Violent Crimes Unit Director Riaan Booysen, who arranges for a magistrate to meet them at the Bellville Magistrate's Court at this late hour. Justice doesn't stick to office hours, and those who live their lives in its pursuit know this all too well.

While Morris and Woest wait for the call to confirm that the magistrate is ready for them, Woest is talkative. He tells Morris that Theys is lying, and that he wasn't the mastermind. It was all Theys's idea. He was just following along.

At 10.30pm, Woest gives a full confession to Magistrate van der Merwe. He is then taken to New Somerset Hospital – where Quinton Taylor had three weeks before fought for his life, and won – to have blood and hair samples taken. He is also checked for injuries.

Twenty hours after he and his colleagues met in a supermarket parking lot, Morris is finally on his way home. It's been an incredibly long but successful shift and, as he drives, Woest's confession plays in his mind.

Chapter 15

Confession two

Adam Roy Woest offers his confession on 13 February 2003. (It has been edited for brevity without changing the context or meaning of the statement.)

At some point after moving to Cape Town in 1999, I started to work at a restaurant called Walter's Grill in Main Road, Sea Point. While working there, I befriended a person by the name of Cobus/David. Cobus/David worked as a male escort at Sizzlers.

In the middle of 2002, Cobus/David came to Walter's Grill, clearly upset because he had been fired from his job. During the course of the evening, he got somewhat intoxicated, and amongst other things told me that large amounts of cash were kept on the premises at Sizzlers. Sitting next to us was Trevor Theys. Because David/Cobus was speaking so loud, Trevor Theys was able to hear what he was saying. Trevor Theys was my friend.

At some point, I stopped working for Walter's Grill and went back to George. During October 2002, I came back to Cape Town. Some weeks after my return, I got a job as a waiter at Q4 Restaurant on the Waterfront. As friends, Trevor Theys and I used to go out together often.

I remember once, after the Sizzlers conversation at Walter's Grill, Trevor Theys telling me that he would not mind getting his hands on the Sizzlers money. I initially took it to be a joke. On the morning of January 19 2003 (about 08:00) I received an SMS from Trevor Theys who wanted to know where I was. I told him that I had just arrived home from work and invited him over for a cup of coffee. He came after about 10 minutes later.

While having coffee, Trevor Theys told me that he wanted us to go rob Sizzlers. Again, I thought he was joking. He started to be serious. About 30 minutes after his arrival, he took out a pistol. Theys said this was the pistol I was going to use during the robbery. I have no experience with firearms, therefore can't say which calibre it was. I told Trevor Theys that I did not want to do this. He then reminded me of my fiancée's car accident. Adele, her name, had been previously hit by a car. I interpreted this to be a threat.

I needed to go to the Waterfront, and at about 11:00. Trevor Theys dropped me off there, reminding me to get gloves. I bought these from a chemist at the Waterfront. Trevor Theys wanted us to rob the place that evening, but I had other plans. On the evening of January 19 2003, my friends and I went clubbing at La Med. Trevor Theys phoned me sometime in the evening to know where I was. I told him and he came to fetch me. We then went to my flat.

Trevor Theys had brought with him two firearms and two beanies. I had in my flat the gloves and a tape. Trevor

Theys ordered me to bring along a rope and a knife. I reminded Trevor Theys, again, that I did not want to do this. We finally left my flat.

While on our way to Sizzlers, we stopped in Main Road, Sea Point, at a public phone to make a call to Sizzlers. We wanted to make a booking. I made the phone call, and I was asked what my preference was. I said I'd prefer a blond. If my memory serves me correct, we made the booking for 24:00.

We then went to a petrol station, where Trevor Theys instructed me to fill a two-litre plastic bottle with petrol. After the garage, we went to park the car at Marais Road. While still in the car, we put on our gloves. It was at this point that Trevor Theys handed me the gun. We walked to Sizzlers. I was carrying the two-litre bottle but left it by the security gate before going in.

To the best of my knowledge, we were met at the door by the person reflected in the photo album (referring to the police's album of the deceased). We were taken to Studio 3. While in the room, we were asked if we preferred a blond and if this blond will attend to both of us. I said "yes". The person thereafter left. Upon hearing his footsteps, we took out the firearms. The person reflected in the photo album entered Studio 3. Trevor Theys told the person that it was a robbery, and that as long as everyone cooperated, nobody will get hurt.

While holding this person up, we made our way to the other room. Mr Otgaar was brought in from the room immediately opposite the room we were in before. We asked where the money was kept, and the person I perceived to be the manager showed us and opened the safe. He handed me a bundle of money. It was not more than R2,000.

At this point Trevor Theys instructed me to help him tie our hostages. I gave the rope to one of the persons, I cannot remember who, to do it but Trevor Theys was not happy. He then instructed me to do it personally. Afterwards, Trevor Theys ensured that the rope was tight. He said we must stab them to show them that we meant business. He thought they were hiding some money from us. To the best of my knowledge, I cut Aubrey John Otgaar, Warren Robert Visser and Quinton Taylor with the knife.

While stabbing Mr Otgaar, he tried to fight us off. Theys kicked Otgaar, who then fell to the ground. Theys stabbed him. After this, I left the room and started searching other rooms. Some of the doors were locked.

I went back to where Theys and the rest of the captives were, at which point Trevor Theys told me to pour petrol over the Sizzlers' employees. I did, and they started screaming and crying. At this point, one of the doors opened and a guy with a towel around his body got out running. I believe that person was Sergio de Castro.

Trevor Theys went after him. I followed and entered the room immediately adjacent and found Mr de Castro lying naked on the floor. I then went into another room and found another person, not known to me at the time (Mr Gregory Seymour Berghaus) sitting on the bed.

As one of our captives had asked for a juice, I went to the kitchen to get some juice. While I was in the kitchen, someone attacked me from behind (it was Mr Berghaus). I did not have a firearm with me, but Trevor Theys came to my assistance. He pulled Berghaus from me. Theys hit

Mr Berghaus with his gun on the head. During the scuffle that ensued between them, they moved from the kitchen to the bathroom. At that point, shots were fired and I don't know whether it was intentional or by accident.

As I was walking out of the kitchen, Theys gave me back my firearm. We then went to the corridor, back to the room where the remaining people were. By the doorway of the room they were in, De Castro was lying on the floor. Theys pushed me into the room. I realised that Mr de Castro had been shot. Without any warning, Trevor Theys started shooting our hostages from the left.

I started shooting from the right. And as I recall, I shot Aubrey John Otgaar, Warren Visser and Quinton Taylor. After this, we exited the premises.

I was then arrested. Subsequent to my arrest, I made a confession. I even pointed out evidence and attended an ID parade. Although I asked to speak to an attorney before making of the confession (and the pointing out), I was told by the police that it is better to make the confession and pointing out first before speaking to a lawyer. However, I do not contest the admissibility of my confession. Although I cannot erase what happened on the night of January 19/20 2003, I apologise for my actions.

Chapter 16

Three versions, one truth

In any criminal act involving multiple perpetrators, it is common for versions of events to differ. The extent to which these versions differ often correlates to how badly each offender wishes to minimise their involvement in the crime. In criminal pairings, each party almost always attempts to paint the other as the main perpetrator. Sometimes it's difficult to determine which party is telling the truth because there may be no survivors. Physical evidence can go some way in proving who did what but rarely answers all the questions.

The confessions by Theys and Woest are textbook finger-pointing. Neither wants to take responsibility for being the mastermind, and both claim to have been the submissive party. Of course, this isn't possible. They may have been evenly matched in the planning and execution of the crimes, but their confessions cannot both be accurate. One of them is lying to some extent. The question is, which one?

In most criminal cases, it makes a negligible difference

from a legal perspective. The two parties are equally guilty in the eyes of the law. The same applies in this case, of course, but there is a third version – at least for part of the account. So, it is possible to compare the offenders' versions to that of the surviving victim, Quinton Taylor, and the physical evidence.

Woest and Theys agree on the fact that they were friends and that the original idea to rob Sizzlers emerged at Walter's Grill. Both say that the information had come from a former Sizzlers employee. This claim holds water: many commercial and domestic robberies involve a dissatisfied worker.

From here, their versions diverge significantly. Both claim that the other was the driving force in keeping the idea going. Both claim they were "joking" when they initially agreed to the robbery, and that the other party kept pressing them to do it. Woest even claims that Theys threatened Adele. Theys seems to blame his alleged easily manipulated state of mind on his ex-girlfriend's infidelity and only mentions being afraid of Woest much later.

Neither man ever mentions the fact that Woest's girlfriend left for Johannesburg on 18 January 2003 – the day before the massacre. This is unlikely to be a coincidence. Woest's apartment was their starting point, and he would have been unable to proceed if Adele was home. Failing to mention this leaves a significant gap in the story – whether it was Woest who carefully planned when to commit the crime, or Theys who knew that Adele was leaving town and found it fortunate. If either of them had brought up this point, it would have cast doubt on their respective claims that they had been dragged into the crime.

The timing of the crime was most likely purposeful. Although neither has included such information in their confessions, it's likely that Woest or Theys, or both, milked the dissatisfied former Sizzlers employee for information. This could have included the best times of the week to commit the robbery. When would the safe contain the most money? The answer to this was on a weekend, specifically on a Sunday when the banks were closed and the entire weekend's takings would be in the house.

The men agree on which items were supplied by whom. Both also claim they believed it would be only a robbery and not a mass murder, but neither mentions asking the other why they would need knives *and* guns, as well as petrol, for a robbery.

In Quinton Taylor's statement, he mentions he got the feeling the two men knew Aubrey Otgaar because they called him by his first name. He was correct. Woest had met Aubrey and some of the other victims when they visited Walter's Grill. Adele van den Heever confirmed this, too.

The men allege they made an appointment with Sizzlers so they could access the property while posing as clients. They had balaclavas with them but were not wearing them when they entered the house. They did not seem concerned that their "robbery victims", whom they both allegedly thought would be left unharmed, could identify them.

The last time Woest had worked at Walter's was in October 2002, almost four months before the murders. Aubrey dealt with many people daily, so it is possible he just didn't recognise Woest from Walter's because he hadn't seen him for some time. This might explain why Aubrey dealt with Woest that night as though he were a prospective client, despite also having met Woest's partner, Adele. Any other explanation raises the question whether Woest had previously been a client at Sizzlers. Perhaps this is why Aubrey didn't find it strange that he was there to engage in sex with one of his workers? Whether or not Aubrey or any of the other men that Woest knew recognised him, the fact that Woest and Theys went in without disguising their appearance left them open to being identified later – if they left any witnesses alive.

While neither man can be described as a career criminal, it's impossible to believe that either of them thought they could carry out the robbery, walk out and never be identified by any of the 10 men in the house. Even at this early stage of analysis, both confessions fall apart on that basis alone. The presence of the petrol further emphasises that neither Woest nor Theys could have believed this would be only a robbery. What purpose does petrol serve in a robbery?

As for what happened inside the house, we can compare the men's statements to that of Quinton Taylor – the only person with no reason to lie. Quinton's statement presents Woest as the dominant force in the house that night. Both he and Theys say that Woest was the one who told the victims that they were being robbed. Woest claims Theys made this statement.

Quinton says that Theys gave the rope to one of the other victims to tie everyone up, and when he did not do it well enough, Woest became enraged and told Theys to do it. Theys's confession is vague around this point, but it seems to imply that when Woest didn't like how the binding was going, he had done it himself. Woest claims that after he had given the rope to the victim, Theys became upset and instructed him to tie up the victims himself.

Neither man mentions the gagging of the victims or the fact that Quinton refused to lie on his stomach. Both confessions seem to skip large sections of time and don't refer to any of the clients who arrived during the torture. They were in the house for more than three hours, yet neither statement reflects this.

Woest's angry outburst triggered the stabbing of the victims, Quinton says, as he believed they were concealing valuables. Theys mentions nothing about an angry outburst, but says Woest told him they had to slit the victims' throats. He provides no explanation for the sudden progression from robbery to murder. Woest claims it was Theys who was angry about valuables being withheld and who then made him stab some of the victims.

Quinton Taylor looked Theys in the eyes when he cut his neck. Theys was uncertain of the identity of the victims whose throats he had cut, but from his description of how the victims were positioned, we can ascertain he is referring to Quinton as one of "his" victims. Woest claims it was he who had cut Quinton, which is demonstratively incorrect, and makes one wonder whether he wants to be linked to the survivor in some way.

Taking into account the verification of who cut Quinton's throat and the nature of his neck wound, which was significantly more superficial than those of some of the other victims, it is possible to determine to a relatively high likelihood which man slit which of the victims' throats.

During the autopsies, some victims' neck wounds were found to differ from the others. Such comparisons are not made during the autopsy, but when we look at the overall evidence, Theys's claims about not having carried out life-ending knife injuries carry weight.

Theys inflicted knife injuries on Quinton, Aubrey, Johan and Timothy. Aubrey's injuries were different overall because he had fought back and engaged in a scuffle with Theys and Woest. Johan is the only victim whose autopsy report was not released. Timothy's throat was not slit. He was stabbed three times in the back of the neck.

Marius, Travis, Stephanus and Warren all sustained knife wounds at the hands of Woest.

Quinton says that Woest entered the room with the petrol and poured it over the victims. Theys does not mention this at all in his statement. Woest admits he did this but claims Theys had instructed him to do so.

The part of the massacre that Quinton did not witness involved Sergio de Castro and Gregory Berghaus. Theys and Woest's versions mostly line up regarding the murder of Gregory, but one vital part is missing.

Gregory was the only victim to sustain a gunshot wound to the abdomen. In the confessions, this is revealed to have occurred during a struggle between Theys and Gregory. This fits with the evidence, and Theys does not deny shooting him – although he tries to minimise it. Theys tries to paint his initial pistol-whipping of Gregory as proof that he didn't want to fire the gun, but it's more likely that Woest was in the way and he couldn't shoot him at that point.

Woest claims he had gone to the kitchen to fetch something to drink for one of the victims when Gregory attacked him. This seems unlikely, as Theys was in the room with Woest and says he turned around to find

Woest gone. He makes no mention of a victim asking for something to drink.

Perhaps one of the most glaring omissions from both men's testimony, in this respect, is that neither speaks of Gregory sustaining a knife wound to his neck or an additional gunshot wound to the head.

Sergio and Gregory were not part of the bigger group who were lying side by side in the main room. Both Woest and Theys claim they were coerced by the other into slitting the victims' throats. But someone had to have left the room to slit Gregory's and Sergio's throats. They sustained deep incised wounds similar to those found on Woest's victims. Quinton said that Theys had stayed in the room after the knife wounds were inflicted, and Woest had walked out and come back with the petrol. If Woest had truly been coerced into inflicting the knife wounds, why then would he have gone of his own accord to slit the throats of the two other victims?

For Quinton, the shooting started randomly because he was not witness to what was happening with Gregory and Sergio. The shooting of Gregory, according to Theys, is what started the rest of the shootings. He says that after Gregory collapsed, Woest said, "Now it's too late, we have to shoot them." Then Woest shot Sergio, and they both went into the main room to shoot the remaining victims. But Woest denies shooting Sergio. He claims Theys shot the young man and then coerced Woest into helping to shoot the other victims. Although Quinton quickly lost consciousness after being shot, he reported that it was Woest, not Theys, who had first fired on the victims in the room.

At no point in either man's statement do they explain

how Gregory Berghaus came to have an additional gunshot wound to his head. Theys claims that immediately after the "gun went off", resulting in Gregory's abdominal wound, Woest took the gun from him. Woest also claims Theys "gave back the gun", yet Gregory was somehow also shot in the left temple – a "kill shot".

Throughout Theys's statement, he randomly claims not to have been in a clear state of mind because of his breakup with his girlfriend. He says several times that he was afraid of Woest. But these words stand out: "Adam was waiting. I don't know for what." The protracted nature of the crime once again goes against the ordinary modus operandi for a robbery. Even Quinton mentions not understanding why the men were taking so long. Woest never refers to the amount of time they spent in the house. He only mentions spending some time going through cupboards and rooms and finding some locked. At no point does he report feeling like they should get out of the house or asking Theys why they were still hanging around.

Woest and Theys are not completely honest in their accounts. Both sidestep issues they may believe would increase their culpability or cast their participation in a different light. Quinton's testimony and the physical evidence support more of Theys's version than of Woest's.

While none of this analysis makes either man more or less guilty of their crimes, it shows that the families of the victims did not get all the answers they deserved from these confessions. It seems likely that Woest was indeed more of a driving force in this crime than Theys, although all the victims died of gunshot wounds and Theys supplied the guns. The men's actions that night do not speak to robbery being their sole motive. They could not reasonably have believed they would get in and out of that house on Graham Road with money but no blood on their hands.

Chapter 17

My fiancé, the mass murderer

Adele van den Heever met Adam Woest in 1997 shortly after she'd left school. She was working as a nurse's aide at a retirement home in George at the time. She and Adam moved in together and got engaged. In 1999, they relocated to Cape Town.

At first, the couple lived in Bellville. Adam had planned to open a computer games shop, but after a few months, Adele accepted a private nursing position in Sea Point and they moved there.

For most of his adult life, Adam had been employed in the restaurant industry, mainly as a server. In Sea Point, he got a job at Walter's Grill. Adele would visit him there while he worked. They befriended many of the customers at the restaurant, including Aubrey Otgaar (Adele knew him as Eric) and some workers from Sizzlers.

Adele described her relationship with Adam as a happy one. She said that she could not point to any aspect of their interactions as a red flag. When pressed, she described

Adam as a "bit of a loner" at times, and his sense of humour as being "on the dark side". Nothing about this ever concerned her or made her fearful of him.

Although Adele never tried to claim Adam was innocent or justify his actions, it is clear from how she spoke about him in the early days that she was struggling to come to terms with his guilt. This is understandable: although most people assume they would know if they were living with someone capable of such a crime, the reality is that most loved ones of offenders are caught off guard.

Many mass murderers might describe their crimes as a case of them "just snapping", but research shows that this is never true. There is almost always some form of "leakage" where the offender will have shared their plans, desires or murderous ideals in some way with someone in the run-up to the crime. Most people will shrug off this leakage. They will think the individual is joking or living in a fantasy world. Although Adele would not have known it, this is likely to be what she witnessed when Adam had his moments of "dark humour" or when he said "weird stuff", as she put it. Of course, unless the leakage is blatant, it is often difficult for an untrained person to pick up on something dangerous and take it seriously.

Adam Woest had a ticking time bomb inside him. Had anything gone wrong at his workplace, there is a significant possibility that he would have carried out a similar crime at Walter's Grill rather than at Sizzlers.

The terrifying truth is that criminals like Woest are extremely good at wearing a mask. Adele van den Heever had to come to terms with the fact that she had lived with Woest for eight years without ever getting to know the "real" Adam.

Adele's interviews with the press show she was going through a grieving process. She was mourning the man she thought she knew and the death of their shared future. At first, she was almost in denial – not about his guilt, but because the Adam *she* knew could not be a cold-blooded killer. "Everyone makes him out to be this monster, but that's not the person I know. He was always willing to help someone out – he'd give his staff meal to someone rather than see them go hungry. I never saw a violent bone in his body."

In later interviews, she seemed to have moved past this stage of grief into anger. She expressed hatred for what Adam did to her and the victims of the massacre. "I hate Adam for what he did. I thought I knew him, but after this I don't think I know him at all. It is confusing to go from so much love to so much hatred. I prefer to think of him as being dead. It's less painful that way."

Adele's mother, Marietjie Kolesky, says her daughter never fully recovered from the trauma. As a secondary victim of the crime, Adele's emotions and challenges were similar to those of the families who lost their loved ones that night.

Many hoped that the person who had probably been closest to Woest at the time of the crime would shed some light on what seemed like an unfathomable event. In interviews with Adele, she clearly wished she had better answers, but the events were simply far too complex for her, or for most ordinary citizens, to understand. In fact, most criminologists will struggle to explain how someone can sustain a long-term relationship, be well-liked at work and, mostly, exhibit few red flags – and then commit mass murder.

This contrast in the man she'd once loved and planned to marry would haunt Adele for the rest of her life.

Adele van den Heever died in 2014 at the age of 33. About her untimely passing, her mother wrote, "My child, Adele, passed away ... due to the trauma that was inflicted on her because of Adam and Trevor's criminal acts. She never recovered from that trauma."

Chapter 18

The journalists

Elsabé Brits

Elsabé Brits was in her early thirties when the Sizzlers massacre happened. As a member of the LGBTQ+ community who had spent a lot of time in the gay bars and clubs of Sea Point, she felt the deep sense of loss and fear among the queer-identifying residents of the area. She was also a crime journalist for Afrikaans news publication *Die Burger*. So, for her, Sizzlers was not just a headline. While her friends viewed the horror from a high level, barely touching the undercurrent of deep grief that ran through those who were involved, it was Brits's job to go deeper.

She describes Sea Point in the early 2000s as "the place to be" if you were gay and wanted to feel relatively safe and not like an outcast. It is all relative, though. For queer people, especially lesbian women, "feeling safe" might only mean that there is a lower chance that men in the area believe in so-called corrective rape. Although Cape Town has always had a reputation as a more "queer-friendly" city than many others in South Africa, not every area and community aligns with this perception. But at the gay clubs and bars in Sea Point, Brits and her friends felt a sense of belonging and could enjoy themselves for a few hours knowing that no one, at least not in the immediate vicinity, would judge them for their sexuality.

Pockets of fear punctuated that period, though – in the form of bomb attacks. In August 2000, Brits was sitting in the Bronx Bar (a gay club) when a bomb exploded in a car on the street outside the entrance. The year before, a pipe bomb had injured nine people at the Blah Bar (also a gay bar). Other incidents had occurred at a bagel store and the Planet Hollywood restaurant – locations not related to the queer community. In total, there were nine bombings in the Cape Town area in the late 1990s and early 2000s. These cases remain unsolved. The group People against Gangsterism and Drugs denied any involvement in the attacks, but it was widely believed that an extremist splinter group of the organisation may have been responsible.

By 2003, when nine men were brutally slaughtered in Sea Point, the bombings had become only painful memories. But, although the Sizzlers massacre was very different from the carnage caused by the explosive devices, it evoked the same feelings of terror.

In her role as a journalist for *Die Burger*, it was Brits's job to report the facts, but she was also a member of the queer community and rumours were rife that there was more to this crime than a robbery gone wrong. While the gay community did not seem to think it had been an extremist act, they believed in the involvement of organised crime. In particular, one rumour was that Cape Flats gangs had gained a foothold in the area and sent a message: "We run the streets here. Don't forget it."

Hard Livings gang boss Rashied Staggie moved to Sea Point from Manenberg on the Cape Flats in 1996. He and his gang then slowly infiltrated the drug scene, ensuring that, block by block, they became the main suppliers of hard drugs in the area. One of Staggie's drug houses was just 250 metres, as the crow flies, from Sizzlers. But, as Brits would discover in her reporting, Aubrey Otgaar, the owner of Sizzlers, did not allow drugs on his premises. He certainly wasn't selling them. Of course, drug dealing is not the only form of revenue for street gangs. The sex trade is equally lucrative for "organisations" like the Hard Livings and The Americans. The former had taken over a hotel in Sea Point around that time and turned it into a sex-work establishment. Mostly, though, the gangs focused on the heterosexual sex trade. It was simpler, with fewer nuances than the gay sex trade.

Many in the gay community in Sea Point, though, were certain it had been a gang hit. Detective Inspector Morris was unconvinced. Other SAPS members thought there was something to it, but the evidence didn't really speak to a gang-related crime. Gang hitmen knew how to get in and out of a scene quickly. They weren't there for information, so they had no reason to torture the victims. Rather, they would access the scene, shoot everyone present (or the intended mark) and leave. They did not hang around for three hours.

While these theories were being touted, Elsabé Brits had

to document and report the facts from the Cape Town High Court. She attended every court appearance of Woest and Theys. Murder and mayhem were not unfamiliar to her. She had seen what human beings could do to each other first-hand and then returned to her office to describe it in palatable terms for public consumption.

Brits had just wrapped up her award-winning coverage of the murder of former first lady Marike de Klerk when the Sizzlers trial started. Viewing this crime through the lens of the people it affected, it's interesting to note how they all came to the case with their own struggles.

In her book *Kyk My in die Oë*, Brits describes how, as she stared at Woest and Theys in the high court and wondered if they were really the monsters their crime suggested, she was dealing with her own "monster". About a year before, her mental health had imploded, and a doctor had diagnosed her with type-one bipolar disorder. Her book beautifully describes her struggle to get help and understand the "monster" living in her head, which finally had a name.

While trying to get her mix of medication right and wrangle her racing thoughts, she was confronted with the horrific scenes shown in court. It was one of the first times, in her experience, that such material was shown to journalists in a South African court. It would usually be reserved for the judge and assessors. She describes it as one of the most shocking things she has ever seen in her life.

For much of Brits's career as a crime journalist, an uncomplicated relationship existed between the media and police. They would sometimes even let journalists access crime scenes once they'd been cleared of danger.

So, crime-scene images were not new to her, but these, she says, were on another level. The brutality exceeded anything she'd ever seen.

No one had to tell Brits that these crimes – both the robbery and the murders – had been premeditated. Her experience as a journalist had confirmed that from the outset. So, when Theys and Woest's initial plea statements were read out and they claimed the murders were a spur-of-the-moment decision, it did not sit right with her.

Although it was not part of Brits's direct mandate to deal with the families of the victims, some of them attended the court proceedings and she spoke to them. She recalls a great sense of unity between those who attended. It was as if only the family members of the Sizzlers victims could truly understand each other's pain.

It was difficult to get any information about the victims, Brits recalls. Some families simply did not want to talk about their loved ones at all. The stigma of sex work and homosexuality added barriers that didn't exist in most other cases. Even today, there is little documented history for many of the victims. With every year that passes, the memories continue to fade.

The thing that stands out most for Brits is that neither offender seemed willing to admit the absolute truth. While this was common in her experience, their claimed motive was ludicrous. No one believed them – then or now.

Not long after the Sizzlers case, Brits left crime journalism. Balancing the trauma with her mental health condition was not conducive to living a healthy life. She is now a science journalist. She covers mostly academic research and current scientific issues, including genetics, astronomy, biology, evolution, palaeontology, archaeology, physics and medicine. Science always behaves the way you expect it to. It's clear and methodical, and its actions in the universe are without personal agenda – unlike those of human beings.

Herman Lategan

Herman Lategan didn't intend to befriend the men at Sizzlers. In fact, he originally went there undercover to write an article about the gay sex trade. He says his life as a young, gay journalist in Sea Point was rather wild at the time and he never wrote that article. Instead, he became an occasional client at Sizzlers and would often just hang out with the young men who worked there.

"Some were young men who came from the *platteland* and tried to make it in the big city. They fell on hard times, and sex work paid the bills. They were all close to each other; they shared the same sadness."

Lategan was dealing with sadness too. In his memoir, *Son of a Whore*, he shares some of the pain and challenges he faced at the time. He saw a lot of himself in these young men, and some of them, as he also did at the time, enjoyed cocaine.

On 20 January 2003, Lategan's phone rang, and he received the news that his friends at Sizzlers had all been murdered the night before. The caller told him to switch on the television. He says he stood frozen with shock. He attended as many of the memorial services as he could, feeling it was the least he could do.

In the days and weeks after the murder, Lategan was

torn between his friendship with the young men and being a journalist. A story like this can make a journalist's career, but Lategan was too shocked and grief-stricken to even think about reporting on the massacre. There was an element of fear, too. "You never know who could take you out," he says.

A member of the queer community himself, he says there was a sense of collective mourning – perhaps not just for those who had been killed but also because Sea Point had been perceived as a place where one could be oneself. Now, though, Lategan feels people have forgotten. "There should be a plaque of remembrance or something, a day, anything. But then, many gay people get killed in South Africa because of rampant discrimination. There should be more awareness, but it seems like rich and middle-class queer people don't really care."

Initially, Lategan believed that the murders may have been drug-related. He thought some of the young men may have owed money to a dealer who had come to collect. Even after Woest and Theys were convicted, he still didn't believe the full truth had been told. "There are secrets we will never know. A larger, darker force was at work here."

He was no stranger to discrimination based on his sexuality and other factors, so he expected the media to report harshly on the victims. However, he was surprised to see the opposite happening. The reporting was quite sensitive, he says.

In December 2003, Lategan published an article about a terrifying experience of his own. Just a few months after his friends were murdered at 7 Graham Road, he experienced a home invasion. Two men broke into his home and held him captive while they ransacked his property. He talked his way out of them harming him, and the men left. Although he doesn't mention it in his article, he admits that while the men were in his home, his mind flashed back to what the men at Sizzlers had experienced. He briefly wondered if that lay in store for him, too. He had a taste of the utter fear and helplessness his friends may have felt. "They didn't have any opportunity to negotiate, though," he says.

Lategan went back to the house on Graham Road some time after it had been cleared out. He describes it as a surreal experience, knowing that this was where his friends had met their end.

He now spends a lot of time in Sea Point. On social media, he regularly shares memories of its residents and some of the restaurants and pubs in the area. Thinking back to how the people of Sea Point reacted to the Sizzlers massacre, he says, "It is a suburb with little sympathy for the underdog. Even more so today. The way they moan about poor people on social media is astounding."

While some residents of the area must have had a "live by the sword, die by the sword" attitude, perhaps the empathy of those who felt personally affected by the murders, like Herman Lategan and Elsabé Brits, made up a little for the heartlessness.

Chapter 19

The law of necessity

On 17 February 2003, Adam Woest and Trevor Theys appear in court for the first time. Magistrate Rashid Mathews conducts the hearing in the Cape Town Magistrate's Court. Each accused is charged with nine counts of murder, one of attempted murder, illegal possession of firearms and ammunition, and armed robbery with aggravating circumstances. Prosecutor David Jacobs appears for the state. Everyone in the courtroom understands that it will be a record-breaking case, one way or another.

Mathews asks the accused if they have legal counsel. Both say they do not and cannot afford to procure private counsel. Mathews advises them to engage Legal Aid attorneys immediately. The charges against them, he says, are such that a life sentence is a possible outcome should they be found guilty. It is in their best interest to ensure they are properly represented.

The defendants agree and put their intent to follow the

magistrate's advice on record. They indicate that they both intend to apply for bail. The case is postponed to 25 February 2003.

The case has made national and international news, and the court is packed with reporters. Family members of Gregory Berghaus and Aubrey Otgaar are there too. They receive a taste of what criminal court proceedings are like – often fraught with delays and frustration. Before the session adjourns, the magistrate warns the media not to publish photographs of the defendants before an identification parade has taken place.

In 2003, social media did not yet have a big impact on criminal cases. Armchair detectives and outraged citizens often feel that suspects are being protected when their identities are withheld or their photographs are not published. It is best practice not to reveal the identities of arrested persons before they are formally charged in court, but even after that, the sharing of photographs can damage a case when a victim or an eyewitness still needs to identify the accused.

Although it was not a common defence in 2003, defendants now regularly use social media coverage to claim that victims and witnesses were unduly influenced. Some are successful in getting evidence thrown out for this reason. There is a thin line between the unintentional impairment of justice and the thrill of "naming and shaming" with a sense of activism.

Thankfully, the media play along, and on 4 March 2003, Quinton Taylor (still known only as Witness 74) is transported under guard to Disa Court in Bishop Lavis for an identification parade. Witness Danie Theunissen, who came face to face with Trevor Theys on the night of the murders, is there too. The police line up 20 individuals – both white and coloured men – with a build and general appearance similar to Theys and Woest. Theunissen goes first and cannot identify any of the men as the person he saw that night. Then, it's Quinton Taylor's turn. It takes just 40 seconds for Quinton to point out Adam Woest and Trevor Theys as the men who had attacked him and murdered his colleagues. As soon as Quinton sees Woest, he begins to shake and hyperventilate.

In the months that follow, the men appear in court several more times. No bail is forthcoming for the pair, and they remain in custody. Both secure legal representation. Woest is represented by Mornay Calitz, and Theys, initially at least, by Christopher Ryke. Within a few days, Ryke steps down as Theys's counsel, citing his former client's inability to keep his story straight as a severe impediment to fair representation. He is replaced by Advocate Nehemiah Ballem.

Due to the nature of the case, both men are sent to Valkenberg Hospital for a 30-day period of psychiatric observation.

In a criminal trial, the purpose of a psychiatric assessment is to determine whether a defendant is fit to stand trial and whether a mental health condition may have affected their ability to tell right from wrong at the time of committing crime. Both Theys and Woest are found fit to stand trial, with no significant mental health conditions that would have affected their criminal capacity.

The case is eventually handed over to Advocate Anthony Stephen of the Directorate for Public Prosecutions. The prosecutor reviews the docket assembled by Detective

Inspector Morris, which is later described as "a model of what a murder docket should be". Stephen asks for more photographs of the scene and aerial shots of the property.

When Morris enters the property in June 2003 to have the photographs taken, the carpets have already been removed. This is not an issue, as Inspector Phillip Jacobs took detailed photographs and videos on the night. All physical evidence collection has long been completed. The pictures Stephen wants are only to give the court a broad overview of the property and the other rooms that had not formed part of the immediate crime scene. The lack of carpets gives Morris an additional piece of information, though. He sees two bullet holes that had not been visible before. Removing part of the floor, the officers retrieve the bullets and add them to their cache of evidence.

It takes more than a year from the time of the arrests for the trial of Theys and Woest to begin. On 3 March 2004, the men are asked to plead to the charges against them.

Adam Woest (Accused 1) pleads guilty to seven counts of murder, one count of attempted murder, one count of robbery with aggravating circumstances, one count of unlawful possession of firearms, and one count of unlawful possession of ammunition. He pleads not guilty to the murders of Sergio de Castro and Gregory Berghaus, claiming he wasn't with Trevor when they were killed.

Trevor Theys (Accused 2) pleads guilty to one count of theft of a firearm, nine counts of murder, one count of attempted murder, one count of robbery with aggravating circumstances, one count of unlawful possession of firearms, and one count of unlawful possession of ammunition.

When defendants enter guilty pleas, the court still has

the option to accept or refuse the pleas. Of course, Woest's claims of innocence on two of the charges would have required inquiry anyway, but Judge Nathan Erasmus decides he can't accept any of the defendants' guilty pleas.

Having read the defendants' plea statements, which closely mirrored their confessions, Judge Erasmus is concerned that each man is claiming to have been coerced, in some fashion, by the other. Section 113 of the Criminal Procedures Act of 1977 prohibits a judge from accepting a guilty plea from a defendant at face value when there is evidence that the defendant may have a valid legal defence against the charges.

"If a court at any stage of the proceedings under section 112(1)(a) or (b) or 112(2) and before sentence is passed, is in doubt whether the accused is in law guilty of the offence to which he or she has pleaded guilty, or if it is alleged or appears to the court that the accused does not admit an allegation in the charge, or that the accused has incorrectly admitted such allegation, or that the accused has a valid defence to the charge, or if the court is of the opinion for any other reason that the accused's plea of guilty should not stand, the court shall record a plea of not guilty and require the prosecutor to proceed with the prosecution."

Because the defendants had claimed they were coerced into committing the crimes, Judge Erasmus rules they may have a defence in terms of the law of necessity. Besides this, he notes the prosecutor has put it on record that the State does not believe most of the contents of the two accused's statements to be true. The judge feels he has no choice but to enter pleas of not guilty to all the charges and give the men the opportunity to present their defences. For the victims' families in attendance, all hope of a relatively speedy resolution dissolves. The judge orders the prosecution to proceed with their case.

Chapter 20

On trial

Mark Hamilton takes the stand as the prosecution's first witness. He testifies about arriving at 7 Graham Road on the morning of 20 January 2003 and the scene of horror he discovered there. He admits to having been a regular client of Sizzlers and says this only made his trauma worse as he had known many of the victims. When asked how the massacre has affected his life in the year since it occurred, he tells the court he has trouble sleeping. He wakes to every little noise. The seeming lack of motive in the case also bothers him. Like paramedic Nick Nevin, Hamilton fears for his own life. If nine people can be savagely murdered so callously at their place of work, he says, is there anywhere that we are safe? As a witness, he says, he feels especially vulnerable. He hadn't seen either of the perpetrators that night, but even after they were arrested, he would constantly look over his shoulder in case someone came to silence him.

Darren Brick, who saw two men leaving the scene of the

massacre in a white BMW, takes the stand next. There was a moment that night, he says, when he thought the BMW was chasing him and his girlfriend. He wondered if the perpetrators thought they'd seen their faces. He tells the court that he will never forget the fear he felt that night.

Witness Jacobus Steyn explains how he'd seen two men running up Marais Road on the night of the massacre. At the time of his initial statement, he did not know that he had witnessed one of his neighbours running to the getaway car. Only once the media reported the defendants' identities did he realise that Adam Woest was one of the accused. He wasn't friends with Woest, but he'd seen him in the building regularly and they greeted each other. That sense of familiarity just intensified his shock and horror. Steyn tells the court how, from his balcony, he'd watched as the pavement outside 7 Graham Road became a shrine to the victims.

As a member of the LGBTQ+ community himself, Steyn had felt both saddened and heartened by the fact that the young men of Sizzlers were being embraced by their community in death in a way they perhaps hadn't been in life. He'd watched people arrive at the scene at night and light candles for the victims. It had felt like Sea Point was in mourning for something it had lost that night – the victims, certainly, but also an indefinable sense of peace that had been ripped away.

One of the most devastating pieces of testimony for the prosecution comes from forensic pathologist Dr Denise Lourens. She conducted some of the massacre victims' autopsies and oversaw the others.

Lourens painstakingly recounts the injuries each victim

sustained and answers the court's questions. She clarifies that all the victims had the same ultimate cause of death: a gunshot wound to the head. Regarding the knife injuries, she confirms that there was a clear distinction between the victims with superficial incisions and those who had been attacked more viciously. Of all the victims, though, the only one who may have died from his knife wounds was Aubrey Otgaar, whose carotid artery was perforated. This would have occurred during the struggle with Theys and Woest when Aubrey attempted to escape.

The court is silent as the pathologist delivers her evidence. Occasionally, a victim's family member leaves the courtroom when they can no longer take the gruesome but necessary testimony. Woest and Theys show no visible reaction to the testimony.

Much is made of defendants appearing unemotional during court cases. One might expect some human emotion to leak through, but defence attorneys will usually advise their clients to remain as detached as possible. The irony of the public's desire to see some form of remorse or horror on the faces of the accused is that an overly emotional reaction will also be met with ire. Facial expressions are picked apart by the media and sometimes interpreted out of context. A grimace becomes a grin; a smile at a loved one becomes heartless humour. The safest approach is a deadpan look, and sometimes that's the defendant's default setting, anyway.

Soon, the pathologist's verbal testimony of horror is replaced by visuals. Inspector Jacobs arranges for the photographs and video he took at the scene to be shown in the courtroom. Almost none of the victims' family members stay for this. A few journalists leave too, their stomach for court reporting not extending to images that will haunt them for months or years. As the inspector gets the video going, the song that was playing on the television at the crime scene fills the courtroom: *Tell It Like It Is*. The judge raises a questioning eyebrow at the LCRC officer, unaccustomed to soundtracks on crime-scene videos. Then, the lyrics drift into the background as the camera moves around the house of horrors. There's an occasional gasp from those who are watching. The judge holds his composure as the bodies of victim after victim fill the screen. Once the video is complete and the judge has a good idea of the layout of the house and where each of the victims was located, the stills are placed on screen. Although those present have already seen these images on the video, they are somehow worse when they are not moving. Theys's and Woest's eyes flick between the screen and the floor.

(The LCRC ran out of evidence markers at one point because there was just too much blood and too many bullets, so the LCRC officers improvised with pieces of paper. It's the South African way. We make a plan. As a result, some victims have A4 pieces of paper propped up against their motionless legs.)

In some images, it's not so much the blood and gore that make the picture disturbing as the everyday things lying about: dominoes scattered across the floor; a suitcase once used for happy trips home to visit family; high-end sports shoes that were undoubtedly the pride of a young man's wardrobe. All signs of life. After the last picture has flashed on screen, those present stare at the word "End" on the final slide – a word with myriad meanings.

During this initial phase of the trial, just before the court adjourns for the day, Trevor Theys puts his hand up to get the judge's attention. Judge Erasmus allows him to speak, and Theys asks to be moved from Pollsmoor to Goodwood prison. He fears for his life in the same prison as Adam Woest, he claims. The judge acknowledges his request but says he has no authority to grant it. He will, however, pass his request on to prison authorities.

Detective Inspector Jonathan Morris takes the stand next. He runs through the process of gathering the evidence, identifying the suspects and making the arrests. He also reiterates to the court that the Sizzlers massacre is the worst crime he has seen in his 27 years of service as a police officer.

When Witness 74 enters the courtroom, the media are not allowed to take photographs or even describe the young man in their reporting. Quinton Taylor has remained in witness protection for 13 months, and he is surrounded by heavily armed guards. Undercover officers are reportedly among those seated in the courtroom too, watching for the slightest hint of untoward behaviour. The young man must remain in witness protection at least until he has delivered his testimony. It will then be his choice whether to return to his own identity and life or to accept a new identity from the witness protection programme. One would think that if Woest and Theys were found guilty, there would be no further threat to him – but many unanswered questions remain, and Quinton's testimony will bring more.

Quinton's testimony on the stand mirrors the information he gave Morris during those painful first few days in the hospital. He describes each moment of the horror he and his friends endured at the hands of the perpetrators he has identified as Woest and Theys. The most intriguing piece of evidence he provides on the stand – evidence that was either not included in the statement he provided from his hospital bed or was redacted – is about a telephone call he believes Woest made during the attack.

Quinton tells the court that while he was lying bound and terrified on the floor and Woest was pacing around the house, he heard Woest make a phone call. At the time, he believed that he was trying to arrange for someone to pick Woest and Theys up from the house. This, of course, would not make sense, given that we know the men had parked the white BMW around the corner. It would later emerge that Woest had denied making any phone calls during the attack. Yet, Quinton is adamant about what he heard.

Despite Woest's denial that this phone call occurred, and there being no mention of phone calls in Theys's testimony, Theys's attorney, Nehemiah Ballem, latches onto this. He tries to suggest other perpetrators may have been involved, which could cast doubt on the prosecution's version.

For many who are present, Quinton's testimony is the first time they've heard exactly what occurred in the house. It helps to dispel some of the myths. The matter of the phone call, though, will continue to fuel public theories that Woest and Theys were part of a bigger conspiracy.

As Quinton wraps up his testimony, his security guards whisk him away. Later that day, he will decide to leave the witness protection programme. He signs himself out, agreeing that he is no longer under the protection of the SAPS. The following day, he is back in court – this time as Quinton

Taylor and not Witness 74. He sits in the gallery among the victims' families, media representatives and members of the public and watches as the rest of the trial unfolds.

The prosecution rests its case after Quinton's testimony. In his closing statement, Advocate Stephen tells the court that the defendants had undoubtedly intended to rob Sizzlers that night. But the fact that they had balaclavas with them and only hid their identities when they left the house pointed to the murders being premeditated, in his opinion.

Neither defence team presents any additional witnesses, nor does Theys or Woest take the stand. Mornay Calitz, for Woest, argues that the murders occurred on the spur of the moment and that his client, at least, had not gone to Sizzlers intending to kill anyone. He tells the court that Woest only took part in the murders after Theys killed Gregory Berghaus and he felt compelled to do so. Additionally, he says, Woest cannot be guilty of the murders of Gregory Berghaus or Sergio de Castro because he was not with Theys when the murders occurred.

Nehemiah Ballem, for Theys, does not add anything to that but reiterates that if Woest was on a phone call during the attack, it points to the involvement of a third party and, in his opinion, casts doubt on the prosecution's entire version of events. With that, the defence rests their case.

Judge Erasmus tells the court that he will hand down his judgment the following day.

In the searing sunlight of a Western Cape summer's day, Quinton Taylor finds himself at the centre of a crowd of journalists outside the court. It hasn't taken them long to put the pieces together, and everyone wants a statement from Witness 74. He agrees to speak briefly, telling those gathered that it is wonderful to have his freedom back, although the violence of that night will always haunt him. One journalist asks why he chose to cast aside the anonymity afforded to him, as he was outed as a sex worker and may face some backlash. Despite the strange and rather insensitive question, Quinton doesn't hesitate in his response.

"I have nothing to hide. Neither did any of the men who died that night. We all had plans and dreams and goals, and we were all just doing the best we could to achieve them."

Chapter 21

Justice?

The morning of 11 March 2004 brings with it a new hope for everyone affected by the Sizzlers massacre. This tragedy has had many chapters and soon, it is hoped, the latest will be over. Judge Erasmus's verdict will not bring back the nine men whose lives were lost that day. It will not heal Quinton Taylor's trauma or his damaged body. But perhaps seeing the two men who committed one of Cape Town's most brutal and infamous crimes found guilty will deliver an element of finality.

Once this chapter closes, there will be room for something else. What that something else is, and whether it will be any better than the deep, gut-wrenching grief of this chapter, remains to be seen.

The feeling in the courtroom is different from previous days. Although Woest and Theys initially pleaded guilty, the judge felt they may have a permissible defence. Their defence teams have not run with the defence of necessity the judge suggested may exist, but that doesn't mean the prosecution is in the clear. Anything can happen – 20 January 2003 has proved that.

Judge Erasmus enters the courtroom and takes his seat. There is a stack of papers before him. His judgment spans 12 pages. He intends to leave no room for error or appeal. This case is far too important to the community and the victims.

He calls on the defendants. They do not need to stand yet, but he wants to make sure he has their attention. He begins with a summary of the scene and holds back nothing in his description of the horror.

"On the morning of 20 January 2003, Mark Hamilton visited the Sizzlers massage parlour, as he had done before. He was met with one of the most gruesome horror scenes imaginable. After seeking help, he returned with the police to find nine men either dead or dying. One can only imagine the stench of petrol, blood and bodies everywhere, the gurgling sound of a person drowning in his own blood, another in a pool of blood trying to kick out of his bonds. This was the aftermath of one of the worst massacres Cape Town has experienced."

A hush falls over the court. Some rub their hands over their arms to fend off the goosebumps rising on their skin. A single tear runs down a cheek.

Judge Erasmus immediately acknowledges that the trial has left everyone with more questions than answers. He references the song that played in the background of the crime-scene video shown in court. The lyrics allude to letting one's conscience be one's guide. The judge has allowed his conscience and the law to be his guide, but he can't say the same for the defendants.

He runs through the charges, naming each victim as he

goes, and then reiterates his decision not to accept the initial guilty pleas. Although a judge would ordinarily summarise the evidence in a judgment, Judge Erasmus states he will not go into everything presented because the defence did not counter anything and presented no evidence of their own. Instead, he summarises the facts as presented by the prosecution, as they are mostly not in dispute. The judge acknowledges some witnesses referred to the victims as "boys", but he prefers to use the word "workers" or "victims". Where pertinent, he uses the victim's full name.

When Judge Erasmus covers Quinton's testimony, he points out that the man refused to lie on his stomach, telling his attackers he wanted to see his death coming. The judge says this reminds him of the words of Che Guevara, a major figure of the Cuban Revolution whose face has become a universal countercultural symbol of rebellion: "I know you. You came to kill me. Shoot, coward, you are only going to kill a man."

Regarding the amount of money stolen, the judge notes there had been about R2,000 in the safe in the main room where the workers had slept, but there had also been a second safe in Aubrey's room. Quinton said he had given Aubrey money for safekeeping, and it was kept there. The judge notes that neither man mentions this money in his statement. He also points out that Theys was in the room with the victims most of the time while Woest was rummaging for valuables. The implication is that Woest may have found the money and pocketed it without telling Theys, but there's no evidence to support that, of course, and the amount of money stolen isn't really important.

The judge then addresses the claim by Advocate Bellam about the possibility of the involvement of others because of Quinton Taylor's testimony regarding the phone call. He states that there is no evidence to support this, and even if there was a phone call, it does not mean that the person on the other end was in any way involved in the murders. The judge also does not believe that the possible existence of other conspirators affects the culpability of the two accused in any way.

He is therefore left with the prosecution's version, which states that the murders were premeditated, and Woest's defence – that the murders were committed on the spur of the moment – to consider. The judge says that Quinton's evidence about the whereabouts of the two accused at the time of Gregory's murder went uncontested, so it is impossible for Woest to claim that he played no role in that murder. Further, Judge Erasmus points out that it is common cause that Woest knew Aubrey Otgaar, at least, and the fact that he entered the house without hiding his identity only leaves the conclusion that he went in knowing there would be no survivors.

The two-litre container of petrol is another source of contention for the judge. Woest's own attorney called it "a means of torture". The judge questions why anyone would want to torture victims of a robbery when they had already found all the valuables. Judge Erasmus also questions the need for the slitting of the victims' throats when the attackers had guns with them. He wonders out loud whether this too was part of the "torture" Calitz referred to, and comments that for him it feels like a tool of degradation.

The three-hour wait on the scene is also on the judge's mind. At this point, he is listing the unanswered questions, all of which add up to the defendants simply not having told the truth. He dismisses Woest's claim that once Gregory was accidentally shot, they "had no other choice" but to shoot the rest of the victims. This, he says, is illogical thinking. If they had really intended to leave the victims alive, it would have been far better to leave behind one injured person than nine dead men.

"We are of the view that the only inference is that the two accused went to the scene with the premeditated intention to kill everyone they found, and robbery," Judge Erasmus says. As such, Woest's plea of not being guilty of the murders of Gregory Berghaus and Sergio de Castro holds no water. The pair acted with common purpose, and they are therefore equally responsible for everything that happened in the house that night, whether or not Woest or Theys pulled the trigger.

Judge Erasmus finds both Adam Woest and Trevor Theys guilty of all charges against them. As a parting gift, he reminds the men – whose sentencing proceedings will begin at some date in the future – that their premeditation of the murders means the minimum prescribed sentence is life.

Chapter 22

Life for a life

Every trial has a sentencing portion, whether or not the defendant has pleaded guilty. In this phase of the trial, the defence counsel can present evidence in mitigation of sentence – age, diminished mental capacity, substance abuse disorders, expressions of remorse and so forth. The prosecution can present evidence in aggravation – the level of violence used, psychiatric reports showing serious personality disorders that would hinder rehabilitation and the like. Affected persons, including secondary and tertiary victims, are given the opportunity to present their victim impact statements to demonstrate the damage the crime has wrought upon their lives.

Therefore, in sentencing an offender, the judge must take several factors into consideration, including the impact on the victim or victims, the impact on society and the possibility of rehabilitation for the offender.

On 15 March 2004, the sentencing proceedings for Adam Woest and Trevor Theys begin in the Cape Town High Court.

The prosecution starts by laying out the factors they believe should be considered as aggravating. Fay Berghaus, Gregory's mother, takes the stand. She tells the court she will never forgive her son's killers. The way he died is simply too horrific for her to even consider, and she is certain it will haunt her for the rest of her life. Fay speaks of the intense fear she and her family has faced that, somehow, Gregory's killers will get away with what they did. She ends by reading a short note written by her nine-year-old grandson – Gregory's nephew. The young boy, who probably could barely comprehend the magnitude of the loss his family suffered, writes, "I am crying here. Why can't you speak to me? I am very scared."

The maxillofacial surgeon who operated on Quinton Taylor also testifies about the severity of his injuries and how he will suffer the ramifications of those injuries for the rest of his life. He says that Quinton is lucky to have survived, considering the injuries he sustained.

One of the most disturbing and revealing moments of testimony comes when the psychiatrist who assessed Adam Woest takes the stand for the prosecution. When asked whether the accused showed any signs of remorse during the assessment, the witness responds that Woest said, "I'm remorseful that I won't get to watch the third *Lord of the Rings* movie in a cinema."

In mitigation of sentence, the psychiatrist who assessed Trevor Theys at Valkenberg, Dr Larissa Panieri-Peter, tells the court that he has an average intelligence and she could not find any history of violent tendencies. The court hears that Theys has six siblings and is the second-youngest child in his family. His father worked as a fisherman and his mother as a caterer. Theys started school at the age of seven along with his peers but had to repeat grades one and two. He left school after passing grade nine. His relationships with his siblings were healthy. He fathered three children and supported them financially when he was working. At the time of his arrest, Theys worked as a taxi driver, predominantly ferrying people in the sex trade to and from their appointments.

While the big question of motive still hangs in the air – although not important for sentencing – the psychiatrist says she could not find that Theys was inherently homophobic. She understood he had suffered a difficult period of grief after his girlfriend left him. He had referred to this several times in his confession, claiming to have not been in his "right mind" because of the pain of the breakup. Dr Panieri-Peter does not feel that Theys focused on his girlfriend's relationship being with another woman as a point of contention, though. She says Theys told her that he was extremely fearful in prison and concerned for his family's safety, as he claimed to have received death threats.

Theys's attorney tries to claim that the murders were completely out of character and that his client had just snapped under pressure from Woest and due to grief from his breakup. Judge Erasmus interjects at this point, asking where in Theys's psychiatric assessment there is any indication that his psychological state was abnormal. Of course, there is no such evidence.

Theys's sister takes the stand next, and her brother's emotions finally get the better of him. Tears stream down his cheeks as she testifies on his behalf. She says that the family is still shocked that her brother has been implicated in the crimes. She can't believe that he would kill anyone. When the prosecution asks her what she thinks should happen to someone who takes nine lives and tries to take a tenth, she concedes that such a person should be punished because that's "not nice".

None of Adam Woest's family or friends take the stand in mitigation. Dr Ashraf Jedaar's pre-sentencing psychiatric report concludes that there is no indication of homophobia in Woest. The doctor notes that Woest's own brother is gay, and the pair has never had any animosity over the man's sexuality. As with Theys, Woest has no history of violent tendencies.

Dr Jedaar shares some of Woest's background with the court, saying that the young man is the eldest of three siblings. Woest told Dr Jedaar that his mother had been caring and supportive, but that his father had a short temper and often used physical punishment on his children. Dr Jedaar found that Woest had struggled with bullying as a child because of his dyslexia, and he had experienced learning and adjustment difficulties in his childhood. He'd spent long periods of time confined to his bedroom to avoid interacting with others, and he left school after completing grade 10.

Dr Jedaar also tells the court that Woest displayed an appropriate expression of remorse, in his opinion, and that he was clearly struggling to reconcile his actions that night with the picture he had of himself.

After a few clarifying questions, both sides rest and Judge Erasmus adjourns the hearing to the following day, when he will hand down his sentence.

Four hundred and 21 days have passed since Adam Woest

and Trevor Theys walked into the house at 7 Graham Road and proceeded to rob, torture and execute nine men. On 16 March 2004, Judge Erasmus calls out their names in the Cape Town High Court and tells them to stand.

Fay Berghaus sits behind the men. Her expression is one of fear. Will the men who slaughtered Gregory get nothing more than a slap on the wrist? In a world where the light of your life can be snuffed out in a second, she has learned to trust no one. Judge Erasmus has expressed his deep horror at the crimes in his judgment, but she will not allow herself to assume this will extend to his sentencing.

Judge Erasmus understands the incredible responsibility he bears. In his preamble, he says, "At this stage, it remains a question of one human being, myself, having to decide the fate of another."

More than a year earlier, Woest and Theys decided the fate of 10 men and countless secondary victims. Now the tables have turned.

Judge Erasmus continues, reminding those present that the Constitution protects human dignity and the right to life and freedom. It is the court's responsibility to uphold these rights for both the accused and the victims. The punishment, he says, should reflect the seriousness of the offence, while also taking into account the rights of the victims, the families of the accused persons and the interests of society.

The judge describes Woest and Theys's crimes as premeditated, well-planned and "unparalleled savagery". He refers to the "extreme callousness and gruesomeness" with which they treated their victims, and he repeats Inspector Morris's words when he testified that, in his 27 years as a policeman, this was the worst murder case he had ever seen. Judge Erasmus rejects both defence counsels' claims that the men had shown remorse. There is a difference between remorse for a crime and self-pity. He tells the men that Quinton Taylor's survival does not diminish what they did to him.

"He was tortured in the same manner as the deceased. The fact that he survived does not detract from the seriousness of that offence. The anxiety of the victims whilst being tortured and assaulted by you is unimaginable. You not only intended to kill, but [also] chose to humiliate them."

Moving on the length of sentence to be handed down, Judge Erasmus explains to the two men that the law stipulates that the highest sentence a court can impose is life imprisonment. He notes the general perception that this means an offender will only need to serve 25 years, regardless of the number of life terms imposed by the court, as all sentences will be served concurrently with the life sentence. He tells the court that he does not, however, understand the law to mean that a person serving a life sentence is automatically eligible for parole.

Despite that, he says, he knows he cannot prescribe to the National Advisory Committee or the parole board. Judge Erasmus notes it is his understanding that the committee will review the sentencing remarks of the presiding judge when the time comes, if ever, to assess the two offenders for parole. He places on record that he trusts his comments will be considered by a committee or parole board at that time.

Then, Judge Erasmus says that if there were a sentence available to him that would allow him to permanently remove Woest and Theys from society, he would hand it down without hesitation.

The death penalty was abolished in South Africa in 1995. Since then, only a few judges have mentioned (or implied) in their sentencing remarks that they wished they had a stronger sentence to hand down. The last time a judge publicly mentioned this was in 1997 when serial killer Moses Sithole was convicted. Woest and Theys are now in the same bracket as a man who raped and murdered more than 38 women.

In consideration of possible mitigation, Judge Erasmus acknowledges both men are technically first-time offenders. However, where a crime of this magnitude is concerned, he says, this has no bearing on the sentence.

With that, Judge Erasmus reads out the sentences. On count one, theft of a firearm, Theys is sentenced to five years' imprisonment. Thereafter, life sentences are handed down to both men for each of the murders of Aubrey Otgaar, Sergio de Castro, Marius Meyer, Warren Visser, Stephanus Fouché, Travis Reade, Johan Meyer, Timothy Boyd and Gregory Berghaus. For the attempted murder of Quinton Taylor, both men are given 20 years' imprisonment each. Count 12, the charge of armed robbery with aggravating circumstances, adds another 15 years in prison to each of their tallies. For illegally possessing firearms – Theys legally owned one gun but had stolen the other, and Woest was illegally bearing both weapons – three years are added, and the ammunition is charged separately, adding another two years each.

Theys is ordered to serve the five years for theft concurrently with the weapons and ammunition sentences. Both Woest and Theys are declared unfit to ever legally own a firearm again.

Nine life sentences each, plus 45 years for Theys and 40 for Woest. As the judge reads out each sentence, gasps and stifled sobs punctuate the air. It feels like something close to justice – at least for now.

Judge Erasmus thanks everyone involved in the trial and commends the investigation and prosecution teams for impeccable work under difficult circumstances. He has no doubt that every person who worked on the case will have this massacre seared into their memory for the rest of their careers.

Trevor Theys reacts immediately to the closing of proceedings and puts his hands behind his back, waiting for the handcuffs he knows will come. As he is led away, he glances briefly at the celebrating family members and then looks back down at his feet.

Adam Woest sits down after receiving his sentences. He stares straight ahead at the wall, expressionless and unblinking. Eventually, a court officer approaches him and instructs him to stand. He hesitates briefly before complying and is led away. He does not look around as he heads down the stairs.

Theys's brother Andrew is not celebrating. He tells journalists that he believes the case was not properly investigated, and he is certain there were other people involved who could absolve his brother of the crimes. Andrew says he could not have a proper conversation with his brother after his arrest because people were always listening in, and Trevor feared for his family's safety if they dug any deeper.

In a tear-jerking moment, Quinton Taylor exits the court with his arms extended above his head in a celebration of victory. The crowd outside erupts into joyous shouts and applause. Representatives of the Gay and Lesbian Equality Project, the Sex Workers' Education and Advocacy Taskforce, and the Triangle Project are all present in the crowd, which also includes ordinary members of the public and those who knew the victims.

Later, handwritten signs will hang limply, their purpose seemingly served. "Life in prison for gay killers", one reads; "Bring back the death penalty", says another. Life in prison will have to suffice.

In a moment that Quinton is likely to reflect on with sadness, he tells journalists he is overjoyed that the men will never see the outside of a prison cell again. He feels he can finally move on. Like many of the victims' family members that day, he believes that life means life. Tragically, it does not.

Chapter 23

Murder en masse

To really understand crimes like the Sizzlers massacre, it helps to know how professionals analyse the murders of large numbers of people by the same killer.

Sizzlers is considered a mass murder because it fits the internationally recognised definition. When an offender kills three or more people at one location at one time, the crime is labelled a mass murder. This is different from a serial murder. Stewart Wilken, for instance, is referred to as a serial murderer because he killed more than two victims in separate events. Wilken was convicted of murdering seven people in South Africa between 1990 and 1997. The long stretch of time involved points to another difference: serial murderers usually have "cooling off" periods between their crimes.

The third type of murder involves a killer travelling to different locations in a short period of time to kill two or more victims. This is known as a spree murder. A South African example of a spree murder is the 1983 crimes of

Charmaine Phillips and Pieter Grundlingh. The Bonnie-and-Clyde-style couple killed four people across the country.

The Sizzlers massacre falls into the mass-murder category, but it doesn't fit neatly into many other boxes.

Criminologists place different types of mass murders into three categories. When a killer is related to their victims, the mass murder is called a familicide. Sadly, familicides are increasing in frequency in South Africa. An example is the Van Breda family murder in which 20-year-old Henri van Breda attacked four members of his family with an axe in 2015. Only his sister, Marli, survived.

When a mass murder is connected to ongoing criminal activities like robberies, gang culture or drug dealing, it is classified as a criminal-related mass murder. Many mass shootings in South African taverns fall into this category.

Mass public murders are the third category. These usually take place at concerts, schools and shopping malls, such as the Westgate shopping-mall attack in Kenya in which 71 people lost their lives in 2013.

If we focused on the robbery objective in the Sizzlers massacre, it would fit the second classification.

In any crime, motive can be complex to ascertain. The reason for committing a crime may appear obvious on the surface, but many factors affect the offender's true motivation. Additionally, there can be different motivations for different aspects of the crime. The reason for killing, for instance, may be driven by one factor and the victim selection by another.

Those who murder their family members for insurance payouts commit the crimes for financial gain. Their victim selection, though, is driven by a different motive: ease of access. This differs from family annihilators who are also killing their family members but not for financial gain. The motive for a crime can even be a mixed bag: it may present as financial in nature, but the murderer also gained some intrinsic psychological benefit from the crime in terms of power and control.

In *Extreme Killing: Understanding Mass and Serial Murder*, researchers James Alan Fox and Jack Levin lay out five major motivations for mass murder. The first is power. Mass murderers who are driven by a desire for power in their crimes seek to dominate and control their victims. They will often be militaristic in their presentation and display a need for superiority, attention and recognition. The attacks carried out in July 2011 by Norwegian mass murderer Anders Breivik, who murdered a total of 77 people in Oslo and on the island of Utøya, is an example of this type of motivation. Breivik was highly militarised in his actions, the clothing he chose and his planning.

The second motivation for mass murder is revenge. In school and workplace shootings, the offender often wants to correct a perceived wrong enacted against them. Revenge-motivated mass murders tend to appear quite different on the surface because the offenders' perception of their victimhood is often not based in reality.

Other examples of revenge-motivated mass murders are a spouse murdering their children to get back at their partner for something, or an ex-employee carrying out a mass shooting at their previous workplace. Hate crimes can also fall into this category, depending on what the offender believes to be true.

Loyalty is the third major motivation that Fox and Levin

supply for mass murder. This usually manifests as loyalty to a specific belief system or ideology. The belief system can belong to a group or it can be something that the individual has come up with themselves. Cult murders, like the Manson Family murders in the US, often fall into this category.

The next motivator is closely aligned to the loyalty-related motivation. Terror attacks are usually committed by individuals or groups who set out to create social discord to further their cause – which may include ideologies or political beliefs. A local example is the so-called Wit Wolf case in which Barend Strydom murdered eight black victims in November 1988 in Pretoria in a targeted attack he claimed was in support of his political ideology.

The final major motivation for mass murder is profit. This motive is evident in cases where the perpetrators kill the victims primarily for financial gain. Assuming a robbery motivation, the Sizzlers mass murder would fall into this category.

In many of these examples, it's clear that although one motivator stands out, there are several motivations at play at the same time. They all contribute to a greater or lesser degree and can be linked to the victims' injuries or the killers' modus operandi.

The easiest way to understand the true motivations behind the Sizzlers massacre would be to compare it to a similar case. However, the specific elements of this crime – the mass murder of members of the LGBTQ+ community who were also sex workers, with robbery claimed as the motive – do not match any other publicly documented crime internationally.

Some mass murders are classified as either hate crimes or having another ideological motive.

In the early hours of 12 June 2016, 29-year-old Omar Mateen targeted the popular gay nightclub Pulse in Orlando, Florida. In what was the deadliest US mass shooting at the time, Mateen shot to death 49 people and wounded another 53 before taking his own life. It initially seemed that he had committed the crime in allegiance to the Islamic State of Iraq and Syria (ISIS). Mateen, who was born in the US to Afghan parents, made this claim during negotiation phone calls with the police and conversations with hostages. Police established that he had known people with links to ISIS but could not find concrete ties between him and the Islamic organisation. Although he was born into a Muslim family, those who knew him said he was not devout and regularly drank excessive amounts of alcohol. While the devout following of religion is not a prerequisite for radicalisation, Mateen's alleged steadfast commitment to ISIS only seemed to have emerged in the days before the Pulse shooting.

Although this seemed to be a hate crime, investigators who delved into Mateen's history could not find any real instances of homophobic behaviour. In fact, many members of the LGBTQ+ community came forward after the crime to say that they recognised Mateen from engaging with him on queer dating apps. Investigators said they could find no proof of this either, but some of Mateen's family members claimed that he'd had homosexual encounters. One even alleged that agents from the Federal Bureau of Investigation had warned them not to leak this information to the media. In addition, released records of

Mateen's search history showed that on the night of the mass shooting, he had searched for "downtown Orlando nightclubs" – but there was no evidence that he had selected Pulse because it was a gay nightclub.

Mateen, as opposed to Woest and Theys, had a violent and abusive background. The FBI had flagged him several times for making terroristic statements on social media. His first wife, who left him after only a few months of marriage, described him as "incredibly violent and abusive". It's likely that, had Mateen gone to trial, his initially claimed motive would have been proven untrue – similar to the Sizzlers case.

The only criminal case that comes anywhere close to the Sizzlers massacre in circumstance and claimed motive is not a mass murder but a case of serial murder.

For four months in 1993, a serial murderer terrorised the LGBTQ+ community in West Yorkshire. Five gay men were found murdered in their homes in crimes that sometimes appeared to be accidental deaths during acts of sadomasochism or autoerotic asphyxiation. English police initially did not link the cases, but after pressure from the queer community, 39-year-old Colin Ireland was arrested for the series of murders. He eventually confessed to the murders but claimed that he was neither gay nor homophobic. He said he had only selected members of the queer community because he knew they were vulnerable people whose murders would not attract much attention. Ultimately, he claimed his motive was robbery, and he killed the men to avoid identification. Forensic psychologists who assessed the case found that Ireland was a classic serial murderer whose motive was intrinsic and focused on power and control, and the financial gain was only an added benefit for him.

The psychology of mass murderers differs from that of serial murderers. Perhaps the easiest way to explain the difference is by understanding the nature of these crimes. Mass murder is a premeditated explosion, whereas serial murder is a slow, sustained burn. Although all types of criminals may escalate their crimes, mass murderers are more likely than serial murderers to have only a light criminal record or none at all. Serial murders often have a sexual motivation (whether literal or perceived), so it is common to find sex crimes in the history of a serial murderer. It is easier to map out the progression of a serial murderer by looking at their history than it is to understand how a mass murderer developed. Colin Ireland's history is awash with criminal activity and escalating violence. Adam Woest and Trevor Theys, however, have none of that in their histories. To the untrained eye, they seem the least likely candidates to commit mass murder.

Doctor Gérard Labuschagne has been a practising clinical psychologist since February 1998. After completing his internship at 1 Military Hospital in Pretoria in 1997 and qualifying as a clinical psychologist, he worked at Weskoppies Psychiatric Hospital as a consultant clinical psychologist (with a joint appointment as a lecturer in the Department of Psychiatry at the University of Pretoria) for three-and-a-half years before taking up a position in the SAPS in October 2001. During his 14 years with the SAPS, Dr Labuschagne headed up the Investigative Psychology Section (IPS), which is responsible for helping the SAPS investigate psychologically motivated crimes such as serial sex offences, murders and stalking. After leaving the SAPS, he started his own company, L&S Threat Management, which focuses on workplace threat management. He also leads the African Association of Threat Assessment Professionals, a nonprofit organisation that educates professionals and the public about threat assessment and management.

Dr Labuschagne says that the public and Theys and Woest's friends and families may have been shocked by the men's overnight transition from ordinary citizens to mass murderers, but he sees such behaviour all the time.

"I have seen very so-called normal people do [terrible things]. I think in society and in the media, it is very much 'there has to be more to this' … 'This has to be a hate crime. It has to be something bigger. It has to be a gang-related hit.'

"And I think that's partly society wanting [the motivation for crime] to be that, because it makes them feel more comfortable if they can identify it. Giving it a label – like saying the person committed this very violent act because of schizophrenia or something else – makes us feel a bit more comfortable."

In previous interviews regarding mass murder, Dr Labuschagne has reinforced the fact that although such changes may seem sudden, there are always small and sometimes overt signs that something is wrong. Importantly, these signs do not always mean someone will commit a crime like the Sizzlers massacre. Far more often, emotional instability or threats of violence are indicators of possible self-harm. Either way, if more professionals and members of the public learn to identify these signs, the individual can get help and the ultimate outcome might be thwarted.

Having two offenders involved in a mass murder is uncommon but also depends on the motive. In mass murders motivated by domestic violence, ideology or terrorism, often only one perpetrator is involved. Those motivated by robbery may include more than one offender. All circumstances also have their exceptions, such as the Columbine High School massacre in Colorado in the US where Dylan Klebold and Eric Harris murdered 12 of their fellow pupils and one teacher before taking their own lives. It was initially seen as a case of revenge-motivated murder, but the conclusion stated that it was a mix of revenge, ideology and suicidal ideation by the offenders. In most cases where two offenders commit a mass murder, there is a basic link between the two. Klebold and Harris, for instance, attended the same school.

Adam Woest and Trevor Theys, though, could not have been more different.

Chapter 24

Killer friends

On the face of it, it seems unlikely that police would ever have linked Adam Woest and Trevor Theys had it not been for Quinton's eyewitness account and Trevor's confession. The pair were the most unlikely of cohorts and different in almost every way.

Woest and Theys met at Walter's Grill when Woest worked there as a server and Theys was a customer. Theys often hung around at the restaurant while he was on duty as a taxi driver for escort agencies. While he waited for his next fare to come through, he would drink at the bar and he and Woest became friendly. As we know, Woest knew many of the young men who worked at Sizzlers and the owner, Aubrey Otgaar.

Theys's involvement as a taxi driver in the sex industry is an interesting connection that has seemingly never been fully explored. In one of Quinton Taylor's media interviews in the years following the massacre, he mentions that Theys had occasionally driven Sizzlers' workers around. It is unclear how Quinton knew this, as he had not recognised the man on the night. An old friend of Aubrey's – a female member of the queer community that he trusted and with whom the workers felt comfortable – ordinarily performed this function. It is possible that Theys could have filled in occasionally, but that presents another question: surely Aubrey would then have recognised him?

Either way, the fact that Theys understood the sex trade while Woest was friendly with many of the workers could have been an additional point of connection between them – especially when, as the men alleged, a spurned Sizzlers employee had run his mouth about how easy it would be to rob the place.

In criminal partnerships – whether romantic or platonic – post-crime analysis often finds one member of the partnership to have been demonstrably dominant over the other. There is often some coercive control in these types of partnerships, but usually it is just a case of the more manipulative partner using the other person's weak points to their benefit.

Adam Woest needed resources from Trevor Theys to commit their crime. Theys supplied the two most important tools – the guns and the getaway vehicle. It is also likely that Woest knew that controlling a large group of people on his own would be almost impossible, so he needed a partner. Whether he specifically selected Theys because the man was not particularly confident or dominant is difficult to say. Woest knew many people through his work as a server, and he had friends with whom he went to nightclubs and bars, but it would take a specific type of person to agree to this crime. Perhaps Theys just fit the bill most closely.

Theys was not doing well financially and shared his woes with Woest over drinks at the bar. This revelation could have been why Woest decided to draw the older man into this plan.

Dr Gérard Labuschagne was called in shortly after the arrests to interview Woest and Theys, in the hope that he could glean some additional insights into the case. He describes their first-hand interactions as "brief and not particularly enlightening", but he does provide some interesting information.

Trevor Theys stuck to his original story when speaking to Dr Labuschagne. He found Theys to be remorseful and said the soft-spoken man often became emotional and cried. In their conversation, he didn't pick up anything from a criminological perspective that he thought could be useful to the investigative team. Theys came across as extremely anxious about his own safety and that of his family. Dr Labuschagne emphasises that although Theys may not have presented with any particularly concerning personality traits during that interview, he was clearly a dangerous individual. Anyone who can kill nine people, regardless of whether their role was dominant or submissive, is a risk to society.

For Dr Labuschagne, the true riddle of the case presented itself when he met Adam Woest. He describes Woest as effeminate, chubby and someone who would not stand out in a crowd. His exterior presentation, however, did not match his interior world, Dr Labuschagne found. Despite already having confessed, Woest was noncommittal about the events of that night in his conversation with the psychologist.

Later, when Woest met the assigned psychiatrist to conduct his formal assessment, he claimed not to remember anything that happened during the massacre. Rather than seeming remorseful, he came across as glib and superficially charming. Regarding Woest's behaviour during his stay at Valkenberg Hospital for his psychiatric assessment, Dr Labuschagne says he was told the man appeared to think he was in a hotel. He constantly complained about everything happening on the ward, from the food to the other patients and even the entertainment on offer. Ordinarily, forensic psychiatric patients do their best to make a good impression and won't complain even if they aren't entirely happy with something. Woest didn't seem to care if he appeared entitled and demanding. Rather, he appeared to think he deserved far better than the other patients and couldn't understand why the staff didn't agree. Dr Labuschagne says these seemingly minor aspects of Woest's behaviour provide clues to his true inner world.

While Woest would later be diagnosed with a clinical mental health condition (which would not have affected his behaviour at the time of the crime and therefore is not relevant to his legal guilt or innocence), the traits Dr Labuschagne and other experts and professionals picked up in him may be linked to one or more personality disorders.

Personality disorders are incredibly common in incarcerated offenders, and Woest's manipulative and entitled behaviour, superficial charm and lack of empathy – as well as the ease with which he lied – all point to a possible antisocial personality disorder. Again, this is not in any way a legal defence for his crimes. Most people living with personality disorders are not incarcerated offenders and may never commit a crime in their lives. They certainly do not murder nine people.

Despite his extensive experience with thousands of offenders, Dr Labuschagne notes that even he found the criminal pairing of Theys and Woest to be "weird". He says their age difference and huge disparity in background – and the fact that both had no criminal record to speak of – made for a partnership that he, as a seasoned detective, would never have expected.

Part of Dr Labuschagne's threat assessment work now involves analysing mass murders across the world to understand how the offenders arrived at that point. He's seen a variety of circumstances and motives leading to mass murder – and, in his opinion, there is no way the Sizzlers murders were a spur-of-the-moment decision.

He acknowledges there are instances where situations escalate and things get out of hand. However, the preparation, the choices made along the way, the length of time spent on the scene and the elements of torture in the Sizzlers massacre do not speak to an unintended escalation, he says.

Woest and Theys had walked into 7 Graham Road knowing that they would walk out with blood on their hands. Maybe Theys had convinced himself it wouldn't be necessary, or perhaps he didn't mind either way. Woest, on the other hand, had been entirely intentional about what he wanted to happen. Yes, he would get some money too, but for Woest, that was undoubtedly just a bonus.

Chapter 25

Scars

When asked where he's originally from, Quinton Taylor says he doesn't really know. "It's a bit of a tricky question," he says, painfully aware that for most people it's a simple answer. "I grew up in a few different children's homes in the Orange Grove area."

It's been years since he dragged himself from 7 Graham Road in Sea Point to the petrol station and collapsed on the ground, begging for someone to save his life. Today, Quinton is tanned with a slightly muscular build and a smile that almost always reaches his eyes.

He is far more comfortable speaking about his recovery from his injuries and trauma post-Sizzlers than discussing his life before the event. As for the massacre itself, he has repeated the nightmare so many times to so many journalists and television crews over the years that it seems pointless to ask him to do so again. He seems to have far more interesting things to discuss, anyway. Occasionally, when topics related directly to that night come up – the paramedic who attended the scene, some of the evidence – his eyes briefly darken and he looks away. If not for these moments, you would never know you're sitting in front of a man who lived through a massacre.

Quinton's childhood was undoubtedly not ideal – but, he says, when it's all you know, it doesn't seem that bad. He understands now that being in a family environment may have been more beneficial for him, but he wasn't dealt those cards. When he was 14 years old, he was adopted by a family. He says the family was well off but the transition was difficult. He struggled at school, and his adoptive parents decided he would do better in a trade school. Instead, Quinton struggled even more and became nomadic, moving around the country several times before coming back to the family's home, only to repeat the cycle again.

He describes himself as "very lost" during his late teens and early 20s. He lived in a commune in Knysna at one point and then went back home to visit his adoptive parents.

Somewhere along his travels, a young Quinton was promised a piece of land for R10,000. He now knows it was a scam, but back then, he thought that if he could borrow the money from his family, he might finally have a place to call home. So, he went back home to see if his parents would loan him the money. He used the last of his own money to get there, so when his father refused, Quinton was in a quandary. Staying with his family was not an option. As he puts it, "My parents have really nice aspects to them, but they have really brutal aspects to them too. They basically adopted me when I was 14 and kicked me out when I was 18." He was expected to make his own way in the world and had been doing just that, one way or another, until that point.

After his dad refused to help him with a loan and he'd used every cent he had to get to their house, he found himself walking the streets of Sea Point. He now recognises he must have cut a pretty sad sight because it wasn't long until he was approached by a man he knew as Eric – Aubrey Otgaar. Aubrey asked Quinton whether he had anywhere to stay and listened to his story. While he now acknowledges it sounds like odd behaviour for a man to pick young men off the street, he later discovered that Aubrey did this occasionally. He always made sure the boys knew what Sizzlers was upfront. They could stay a few days to get them off the streets, and there was never any assumption they would take part in the sex work. Quinton was, however, not shocked that Aubrey ran a sex-trade establishment. He'd briefly worked in one before.

A few years before meeting Aubrey, Quinton had found himself in another difficult situation, one he describes as "a choice between two bad options". He had to choose between sleeping on the street or earning money in the sex trade. He chose the latter. Toward the end of 2002, when Aubrey offered him a place to stay for a while, he made that choice again.

Quinton saw the work as a means to an end at the time, and still does. However, even the brief periods he worked in the sex trade had a deep impact on his psyche, he says. It affects how you see sex and your own body. He says he has always identified as bisexual, and the assumption that all the men at Sizzlers were gay bugged him – although he's not sure why.

The men who died that night are never far from his mind. Even though he was only there for a short time before the massacre occurred, Quinton says he had already started thinking of the other workers as friends. "You feel a camaraderie. You feel a connection because you're all going through your own struggles," he says. His voice becomes softer as he adds, "And they're all good people. They're all decent people."

Quinton is convinced that there was more to Adam Woest's motivation than money. "He radiated anger the whole time," he says. "Any time Trevor tried to say something to calm us or extend kindness, it was always Adam who snatched it back or told Trevor to stop." His brow furrows as he tries, more than two decades later, to understand the incomprehensible. "I can't explain it. It was just like he hated all of us for existing."

After 13 months in the witness protection programme, which was almost the most harrowing part of the experience, Quinton Taylor raised his hands in jubilation outside the courtroom – and then everyone just seemed to go back to their lives. The families returned to their respective homes across the country, the journalists moved on to the next story and Sea Point slowly cobbled itself back together. Quinton Taylor had to figure out who he was, post-Sizzlers.

"I don't want to say that I'm glad this happened to me," he says, "because there are nine guys who didn't make it out of there. But I can say that, maybe because of who I was to begin with, the attack actually made me a stronger and better person."

During the interview, he radiates confidence. He's

comfortable in his own skin. While this does come with age – and, at 45, many people feel less self-conscious and more liberated – Quinton's demeanour is different. Most people, even if they are confident in their own abilities, still fear the unknown, especially in a country with a crime rate as high as South Africa's. No matter how successful you are, your confidence is not bulletproof. Just around the corner, there could be something that will completely change your life. Quinton Taylor has already looked the worst of humanity in the eyes and survived.

Soon after the crime, Quinton recognised that his life had been reset. His previous ways of thinking, which he admits were based on fear and anxiety, no longer existed. "I could choose," he says, "if I wanted to be a puddle of fear and scared of my own shadow or if I wanted to use this experience to benefit me." He chose the latter.

Quinton has never forgotten that his refusal to lie face down saved him, even though doctors could not fully explain it. "I wanted to look my killer in the eye," he says, the defiance still thick in his throat, "and I think that's how I look at life now. Looking away, running away, doesn't help. You always have a better chance at surviving when you look the monster in the eye."

He understands this is an insight that came after his experience and not something he knew in the moment. "I definitely thought I was going to die," he admits. "I was actually a bit surprised when I woke up."

More than anything, Quinton says, he wants to use his story to encourage people. He wants those who have been dealt a bad hand in life to know that if he could make it through what happened to him, they can, too. "It's hard work," he says. "It's easier just to sit back and be the victim. I'm sure no one would be surprised if I was an alcoholic or a drug addict or if my life had gone totally off the rails after Sizzlers, but what would be the point of that, because then I've given those guys another life? Then they eventually got their tenth victim." That is clearly not going to happen. Not if Quinton can help it.

Woest and Theys going to prison was a big part of Quinton's healing process. Without that, he says, he doesn't think things would have turned out well for him.

For almost two decades, he and the other victims' families lived with the hope that neither offender would ever see the light of day again. For one offender, though, the clock was ticking towards a very different reality.

Chapter 26

Treading water

After serving just five years in prison for his crimes, Trevor Theys died in 2008. The heart condition that had troubled him throughout his life finally ended it while he received treatment at Tygerberg Hospital. Upon hearing of his death, his family had to act quickly to bury him before the press found out. They were terrified that his funeral would become a spectacle.

In all types of grief, whether caused by violent crime or not, many of those left behind express disdain for the word "closure". Where violent crime is concerned, the word is commonly used by court officials, police officers, journalists and the true-crime-consuming public to describe what they think will happen once a sentence is handed down. The family will finally have what they need – information, admissions, answers – to put their loved one to rest, both literally and figuratively. Yet, anyone who has lost a loved one to murder or even survived a violent crime knows that "closure" is a placating fallacy. Undoubtedly, seeing an offender admit to their crime or go to prison provides some level of psychological comfort, and it can be damaging to the grieving process when that doesn't happen. But the falling gavel does not provide the closure that so many believe it will. The world moves on, but nothing is ever the same again for the victims' families. They just find ways to move forward in this new, maimed version of their lives.

The Visser family chose not to attend the trial proceedings of Adam Woest and Trevor Theys. Some families find this process helpful, and others find it even more traumatising than hearing their loved ones had been murdered. The image of justice that many expect to see carried out in a courtroom differs greatly from the reality. The defendant has a right to due process, and defence strategies can get ugly.

Once the men had been imprisoned, Marlene Visser decided she wanted to speak to them. She had too many unanswered questions. First, a meeting was arranged with Trevor Theys. Fourteen-year-old Leigh told her mother she wanted to accompany her. Marlene initially refused, perhaps horrified at the idea of her innocent teenage daughter within the walls of a prison holding hardened criminals. But Leigh told her mother that she needed to meet Theys to aid her own grieving process, and she couldn't deny her daughter that.

Leigh admits now that it was less about wanting to meet Theys and more about trying to protect her mother. Of the range of emotions Leigh felt after her brother's murder, she recalls her anger the most vividly. Although her mom put her into therapy immediately after the murder, those were early days and Leigh didn't find it easy to work with the therapist to process her emotions. Now, she remembers the almost uncontrollable rage that bubbled up inside her when one of the men responsible for Warren's death sat down in front of her and her mom.

Leigh wasn't sure what she had expected, but the skinny, somewhat pathetic-looking man who started crying almost immediately was not it. "He showed quite a bit of remorse for what had happened," she says. "He cried alongside my mom. He answered all my mom's questions. It's weird to say, but he almost comforted her in that sense. And it's hard to think of a murderer like this, who committed these heinous crimes, as being comforting, but he showed remorse. And I think that's what we needed."

Marlene Visser also went to visit Adam Woest. That meeting went very differently. Leigh did not accompany her mother again, and perhaps it's better that she didn't. Marlene would report that she asked Woest many of the same questions she had asked Theys. She cried and begged for answers. But, where Theys had cried with her, answered her questions and begged for her forgiveness, Woest would not even acknowledge her presence. He sat looking at his hands the entire time. He did not make eye contact, utter a word or shed a single tear. Eventually, Marlene fled the prison, frustrated and horrified at the level of inhumanity she'd just witnessed. When Leigh asked her what Woest was like, her mother said, "The devil lives in him."

Warren's death was a delineating moment for the Visser family. From that moment on, they understood how fragile their lives were and how the monsters were not hiding in the shadows – they were walking around among them.

For a long time, Adam Woest was a literal monster in Leigh's nightmares, an evil entity who followed her everywhere she went. Slowly, she conquered her fear of the man who had committed such horrendous deeds. Now, as an adult, she can hold her head high as she fights to ensure he stays in prison where she believes he belongs – but the fear has not left her. She still sees Woest as a hulking mass of evil with no empathy or trace of human emotion. Perhaps, more terrifyingly, now that he may be released on parole, she sees the dark possibilities of what he might do when he gets out.

After her son died, Marlene Visser could not bear the possibility that she might lose another child and became very protective of her daughter. Leigh had a 9pm curfew until she was 20 years old, and Marlene was in constant contact with her and her other brother to ensure that they were okay. Neither Leigh nor her brother could stand the thought of raising a family and settling down in South Africa. The country just held too many painful memories. So, both siblings emigrated. Her mom supported their decision wholeheartedly. She would feel far better knowing her children were not in the same country as the man who had taken Warren's life – and others like him. Leigh moved to Canada with her husband, but she says it hasn't helped as much as she thought it would. Although she enjoys Canada and it's a great place to live, she misses South Africa. She wants to live in her home country, she says, but she knows she can't. The memories have followed her to her new home, but the demons that remain in South Africa are too overwhelming.

These ripples affect the lives of secondary victims of violent crime for many years after. It is why "closure" is a fallacy. Woest, from his jail cell, and Theys, from his grave, continue to affect lives with their crime.

Joan Versveld, Aubrey Otgaar's mother, also visited Theys in prison. As he had done with Marlene Visser, the man expressed shame at his actions and begged for her forgiveness, which she agreed to give him. The pair became good friends in the years that followed. Theys made a wooden jewellery box for Joan as a gift – a place to keep all that she treasured. Yet, one of her greatest treasures could only be kept in her heart and her memories, and no wooden trinket would make up for the fact that Theys had killed him. Despite this, Joan's family says that she grieved over Theys's death as though she had lost a dear friend.

Chapter 27

The Van Wyk loophole

When Trevor Theys and Adam Woest were handed down nine life sentences in 2003, the victims' families and Quinton Taylor believed this meant the two men would never see the light of day again. The judicial system interprets a life sentence differently, though. Today, if an offender is handed down a life sentence in South Africa, it means that the offender will remain under the auspices of the Department of Correctional Services for the rest of their natural lives. It does not mean that the entire sentence will be served in prison. Offenders who are sentenced to life must serve a minimum non-parole period of 25 years before they become eligible for parole.

It's also important to note that sentences in South Africa (and most countries) are served concurrently (at the same time) and not consecutively (one after the other). Although Judge Erasmus had said that he didn't believe the offenders should ever be released, this does not affect the parole process. The judiciary and the correctional system are separate entities in South Africa.

Becoming eligible for parole does not mean the offender automatically qualifies. It's a privilege they need to earn, not a right. Even if they are released, they continue to serve their sentence and remain the responsibility of the department, but they do so in the outside world.

Had the victims' families been thinking at all in 2003 about the possibility of parole, it is likely they would have had this 25-year period in mind. Perhaps they thought that nine life sentences would automatically disqualify Woest from parole. Some may not have understood that he would serve those sentences concurrently and not consecutively. Media reports often play into this misunderstanding, framing a sentence incorrectly as a calculation of the total number of years – for instance, 225 years instead of nine life sentences.

The families' assumptions would have been incorrect because the timing of the crime and the sentencing actually worked in Woest's (and many other offenders') favour.

Julian Knight is a litigation attorney with three decades of experience. He specialises in, among others, the field of administrative reviews in respect of parole law. He and his firm of attorneys have represented several high-profile offenders in their parole efforts, including Janusz Waluś, who was convicted in 1993 of killing political activist and South African Communist Party leader Chris Hani, and Oscar Pistorius, who was convicted of murdering his girlfriend, Reeva Steenkamp, in 2013.

Knight explains why there are three categories of lifers in our correctional system. "The situation was previously that offenders sentenced to life could only be considered for parole after serving 20 years' imprisonment." But

South Africa has moved through many phases in its history related to politics and recognising the human rights of all citizens. Each phase has affected parole review regulations in its own way. These changes are also not isolated to the time they occur. Judgments made in the past continue to affect offenders and victims today.

Between August 1987 and March 1994, offenders sentenced to life imprisonment had to serve 10 years of their sentence before they would be eligible for parole. But many offenders weren't released until they had served at least 15 years of their sentence.

From 1 March 1994 to 1 October 2004, inmates serving life sentences were required to serve at least 20 years in prison before they became eligible for parole.

On 1 October 2004, the Correctional Services Act 111 of 1998 came into effect. The Act states that lifers are required to serve 25 years in prison before they are eligible for parole. Offenders serving a definitive number of years have to serve half their sentence (a third under the old Act) before being considered for parole. This applies to anyone sentenced after 1 October 2004.

But what of those who were sentenced before that? The Act makes provision in Section 136 for those sentenced to non-life sentences to continue to enjoy the provisions of the old Act – they become eligible after serving a third of their sentence. But, Knight points out, lifers are excluded from this, so offenders who were eligible for parole 20 years into their sentence literally overnight became ineligible until they had served 25 years.

In 2010, one offender affected by this change took the Department of Correctional Services to court, and Knight represented him. Cornelius Johannes van Wyk had been sentenced to three life sentences on 5 September 2004. He was a member of a right-wing group that had carried out terror attacks in 1991, leading to the deaths of three individuals in the instance for which he was sentenced.

Van Wyk's case was essentially that by implementing the new Act, the department had stripped him of a constitutional right that he had enjoyed until that date. He wanted to have the credit system from the old Act reactivated. These credits were earned by lifers for following the rules of the prison facility and taking part in programmes aimed at rehabilitation and other activities seen as positive behaviour on the offender's part. When the credit system was stripped away, the parole eligibility dates of those sentenced before 1 October 2004 were unfairly delayed.

In July 2011, Judge Jan Hiemstra ruled that lifers sentenced before 1 October 2004 would still be allowed to use the credit system. In their cases only, a life sentence would be calculated as 40 years less credits and was reduced to at least 13 years and three months.

The credit system was in place in the Department of Correctional Services between 1 August 1993 and 1 September 2004. So, all offenders sentenced to life in that period would have their eligibility dates advanced in terms of the credits they had earned. Adam Woest was sentenced on 15 March 2004.

Another two judgments were handed down regarding the parole issue. Although they don't directly affect this case, they are important for survivors and the public to understand.

Just before the Van Wyk judgment, another key ruling

was made in a case brought by Paul van Vuren, who had been sentenced to death in 1992 for murder. After the abolishment of the death sentence in South Africa, those on death row had their sentences commuted to life. Van Vuren's judgment allowed those offenders to be dealt with as though their sentences had been handed down with provisions in place in 1992.

In addition to the Van Vuren decision, an offender sentenced to life imprisonment on 5 October 2004 also brought his case before the court around this time. Oupa Phaala had been convicted on 25 September 2004 but only sentenced five days after the new Act came into effect. Phaala's attorneys, instructed by Knight, argued that the court's scheduling of his sentencing hearing had unfairly prejudiced him. In this case, the court found that Section 35(3)n of the Bill of Rights gave offenders who had been sentenced to life the right to have their parole eligibility governed by the date on which the offence was carried out rather than the date they were sentenced. This would only be applicable if changes in regulations would significantly prejudice them.

On 5 August 2011, a letter was circulated to all Department of Correctional Services employees regarding the implementation of these three judgments and what it meant for the offenders in their care. The rulings and Act amendments essentially produced three categories of lifers incarcerated in our correctional facilities today:

Sentenced as from 1 March 1994 until 31 December 1997 (the last of these completes the 13 years and four months minimum on 30 August 2011) who must be considered (for parole) as soon as possible.

Sentenced as from 1 January 1998 until 30 June 1998 (they will qualify within the next six months – after 30 August 2011).

Sentenced from 1 July 1998 until 30 September 2004 (they will qualify later when they complete 13 years and four months).

When the letter was sent, there were 361 incarcerated offenders in the first category, 41 in the second and 4,267 in the third. Woest fell into the last category. At that point, he had served seven years. The clock was ticking.

If the victims' families and Quinton Taylor had thought Woest would be considered for parole after 25 years, they would have had 2029 in their minds as the first time they'd need to worry about him being out and about. Unless they were particularly well-informed, they, like most South Africans, would not have paid much attention to the judgments and regulation amendments in 2010 and 2011 regarding parole. Surely the department would contact them when it was time for Woest to be considered? That was part of its mandate regarding the victims of violent crime in South Africa, after all. As they all went about their lives in 2018, they did not know that Woest was already standing in front of a parole board pleading his case – and none of the victims' family members or Quinton Taylor knew about it.

Chapter 28

Where are the victims?

On 29 October 2018, Adam Roy Woest appeared before a parole board at the Kgosi Mampuru II Correctional Facility (previously Pretoria Central Prison) in Tshwane. The facility has been home to several high-profile inmates over the years, including Annanias Mathe, Radovan Krejčíř and the now infamous Thabo Bester.

Anyone who had not seen Woest since he was sentenced would probably not have recognised him. He had gained a considerable amount of weight, almost all his teeth had been extracted from his mouth, and his skin was grey and pasty. Nevertheless, the moment was a light at the end of the tunnel for Woest. Just 15 years after his arrest and conviction, he'd been advised that he was eligible for parole thanks to the legal actions of his fellow inmates across the country. The process had been surprisingly easy, too. He hadn't had to do any of the stuff his fellow inmates discussed in the common areas when they were stretching their legs and exercising. They had to sit in a room with their victims' families and answer their questions. Woest hadn't had to do any of that. He wasn't sure why, but he was also not going to ask.

For two days, department officials discussed Woest's behaviour in prison and his mental health status. The department's psychologist had raised a red flag, saying that a condition with which Woest had recently been diagnosed required further monitoring before they could confidently clear him from a psychological perspective.

Then, toward the end of the process, on 31 October 2018, someone asked about the victims. Where were they? Had they been contacted? Was a victim–offender dialogue arranged? Blank looks were exchanged. Perhaps, someone murmured, all the victims were uncontactable. There were expressions of incredulity. Of nine victims' family members, not even one could be traced? It was very unlikely – and blatantly incorrect.

Woest's parole was technically declined in 2018. The department said in its official paperwork it was because "the offender should undergo long-term psychotherapy as recommended by the psychologist in order to address his *(listed)* mental health conditions". While this is an important point, even more noteworthy is that the entire parole hearing should have been thrown out. One of the department's most basic of duties – the victim–offender dialogue – had been skipped. It had made no effort to contact the victims or the lone survivor, Quinton Taylor. No one related to the Sizzlers case had any idea that Woest's parole discussion had started.

Later, when Leigh Visser asked about this failure by the department, she was told that victim tracers had tried to find the families but failed. The department could not prove the extent of these attempts except to say that they had even gone to the address on file for one family and found they didn't live there anymore. When asked where they had gone, the department provided the address of the crime scene: 7 Graham Road, Sea Point.

In February 2021, Marlene Visser, mother of Warren Visser, received a telephone call from a representative at the Department of Correctional Services. Adam Woest was eligible for parole in that year and, by law, she and the other victims were being given the opportunity to represent their deceased loved ones and attend a victim–offender dialogue to ask any questions they may have.

Marlene was floored. For weeks, she kept the information to herself before breaking the news to her daughter, Leigh. Over the years, Leigh had tried to follow up with the department on Woest's status. She'd heard far too many horror stories about family members bumping into their loved one's murderers in shopping centres, having had no idea they had been released. Although she lived in Canada, the thought chilled her blood.

All her efforts had come to nothing, though. Many victims of violent crime have experienced this, as getting information out of the department is nigh impossible. As the shock wore off, Leigh made a decision. She told her mother that she would represent the family in the matter. She did not want her mother to go through even more trauma, and she was willing to do this to honour her brother's memory.

Marlene was hesitant to allow her daughter to commit herself to what would be a horrific experience, but she eventually conceded and Leigh went ahead.

During her enquiries, Leigh discovered that Woest had already had a parole hearing. When she learnt of the department's claim that they hadn't known how to contact the victims, she spent a few hours on Facebook, LinkedIn and Google and found many of the family members as well as Quinton Taylor – who was not even on the department's list of victims. The lone survivor who had endured so much and would be well-placed to help the parole board understand the impact of Woest's actions had been erased from their records.

Leigh felt overwhelmed by the task before her. She was the proverbial David facing a Goliath-sized, underresourced system that clearly didn't work the way it was intended. She'd hoped it could be something she could do quietly, with no media involvement. However, she soon understood that in committing herself to the matter, she would have no choice but to sacrifice her anonymity. She looked up the details of South African journalists.

Leigh pulls no punches when she explains what she thinks of Adam Woest. One would expect the sister of a victim to abhor the man, but her opinion of him goes deeper than that. From her description of the Vissers' interaction with Trevor Theys, it's clear that she is still capable of seeing the humanity in these men despite what they put her brother and her family through. She's not blinded by hate and pain. So, when she says that Woest's eyes are "black, empty pits ... void of any kind of human life, any kind of humanity", it strikes a chord.

Many family members of victims of violent crime do not want their killers released on parole – but very often, it is not the punitive aspect of the sentence that matters to them. Most are far more concerned about the preventative measures that imprisonment offers. For those who have already lost so much, their worst nightmare is waking up to the news that the offender has done it again. This happens far more often than it should in South Africa, where the recidivism rate is close to 90 percent. For Leigh Visser, this would be almost as bad as losing her brother again. If Adam Woest were to be released on parole and he killed again, the pain may just be unbearable. She believes this to be a genuine possibility.

"He lacks the basic human trait of empathy," she says. "If you look at any of the huge serial killer cases, they all have the same characteristics of lack of empathy, being completely detached emotionally from themselves. And that's who Adam Woest is, and that is the person that is going to be released into the community again. That is the person that's going to live next to somebody in South Africa. It's a fact. It is a person who is going to be walking in somebody's community, living within a community where there are queer people, and that to me is the scariest thing."

Her reference to the LGBTQ+ community speaks to the enduring mysteries in this case and how these may affect Woest's parole hearing. Many believe that he has never told the whole truth about the motive behind the crime. If the motive is unclear, how can we know that the desires and thought patterns that led to this massacre have been truly rehabilitated?

Chapter 29

Navigating the system

A Department of Correctional Services representative sent Leigh a PowerPoint presentation that explained the victim–offender dialogue. The presentation looked like it was created as an educational resource for the department's employees, not for the family members of victims. In fact, nowhere in the presentation did it mention how the process was supposed to help the victims. The last slide was an image congratulating the department on a job well done.

In theory, the victim–offender dialogue is part of the restorative justice process that is intended to involve the victim in the process of justice and rehabilitation and give them an opportunity to ask any questions they may have. South Africa is not the only country that uses this process – and, unfortunately, it's as hit-and-miss in other countries as it is here. When you implement a process that involves the emotions and mental health of human beings, things will occasionally go awry. A key provision of the victim–offender dialogue is that it should not in any way cause secondary trauma to the victims. If the victims agree to participate, they are prepped beforehand by social workers. Importantly, the department also needs to be sure that the offender is in the right headspace to enter the discussion.

For many victims who have taken part in a victim–offender dialogue, it has reaffirmed their belief that the offender should not be released. They feel it was nothing more than a box-ticking exercise for the offender.

Before Leigh could get to the victim–offender dialogue, though, she had work to do. After the initial contact from the department, everything went quiet. She was terrified that they would again go ahead with the hearing without telling the victims' families. Her numerous calls and emails went unanswered. Eventually, she found someone who would answer her calls – a journalist. Leigh describes Melanie Rice as "an incredible human being" and the reason she finally started getting some answers from the department. Rice contacted the department's spokesperson, Singabakho Nxumalo, explained she was writing an article about the plight of Leigh and the other victims, and asked him to comment. Finally, Leigh started getting some answers.

On 7 March 2021, Leigh started a petition that she plans to present to the parole board to show that Woest's release is not in the interests of society at large. Her petition is addressed to President Cyril Ramaphosa, and the introduction is heart-wrenching and deeply personal. The young woman who wanted nothing more than to deal with her pain privately is now forced to announce this to the world:

Unable to breathe, unable to think, unable to formulate full sentences to you, Mr President, after hearing of this gross injustice. All I can do is to bear my secrets publicly and create this petition in the hopes that it will spark change, not only for South Africans but [also] for young gay men and women around the world, and for the generations that lie ahead of us.

You see, Mr President, at just 14 years old, my perfect vision of the world and humanity was shattered. Suddenly, my world no longer revolved around Barbies and dollies, crayons and puppies, but instead my world became consumed by bogeymen that haunted my every waking minute. At just 14 years old, I learnt the harsh reality that evil lives amongst us. I learnt that people are hateful, scary and full of rage; at least for the longest of time, that was my 14-year-old perspective of all people. You see, Mr President, at 14 years old, my brother's arms were tied behind his back, his throat was slit, he was shot in the head twice and doused in gasoline alongside 9 other gay men (9 South Africans, 1 American), in a crime that South Africa has come to know as the Sizzlers massacre – a day that has haunted me ever since and will continue to haunt me. I tried leaving South Africa to distance myself from the "scene of the crime", leaving everything that I love so much behind, and yet from a distance my secret has continued to haunt me.

Today, the bogeyman comes back to haunt me, but only this time in his more mature form, that of a cold-blooded monster with black expressionless eyes, a monster physiologically inclined toward barbaric violence, a monster whose name is Adam Woest.

There is a familiar name among the 12,000 people who have signed Leigh's petition so far: Marietjie Kolesky. She does so on behalf of her daughter, Adele. She says, "I'm signing because … I am the mother of Adam Woest's fiancée, Adele, at the time of the murder. The trauma that was inflicted upon me and my family with the initial criminal acts and later with my child's death due to this trauma which she couldn't recover from is immense."

She is clear about her feelings for Woest. "Adam is a cold-blooded, soulless being. No heart, no emotions. He will never be rehabilitated. We know the circumstances before Adam and Trevor took those unjust steps to cruelly kill nine people and injure one severely. I know why they did that, and it was not about the money."

Marietjie chose not to participate in the writing of this book. Her family's continued trauma is an example of the ripple effects of the harm generated by violent crime. When a crime involves this many primary victims, the fallout is infinite.

After much struggle, confusion and frustration, Leigh was eventually able to confirm that the victim–offender dialogue would take place in South Africa in January 2023. She booked her flights. By this time, some of the other victims' family members had also confirmed their attendance. Warren Visser's little sister was about to meet the bogeyman.

Chapter 30

Just say you're sorry

Every year for the past two decades, the month of January had been difficult for the Visser family and undoubtedly for every other person affected by the actions of Trevor Theys and Adam Woest. Some years were worse than others, and the nature of grief meant that they never knew when it would hit them. So, when Leigh discovered she and the other victims would meet Woest face to face in the month of January, it seemed both fitting and incredibly painful.

Leigh arrived in South Africa and met the other victims. They were bonded by the event they would have rather forgotten, living with pain that most people would not understand.

Leigh was busy in the run-up to the victim–offender dialogue. Although she had learned to live with the trauma of her brother's murder, it had never left her. Over the years, she suffered nightmares in which Woest was a faceless monster hunting her. She experienced panic attacks and, at first, did not know what was happening to her. She tried therapy but felt it made it worse.

However, she refused to waste the opportunity to face her brother's killer. So, she got to work preparing herself by talking about the crime, over and over, forcing herself to think about it, and imagining what the dialogue would be like. When she could recite all the details of what happened to Warren without having a panic attack, she felt she was ready. There was still no way to know, though, exactly what would happen when she sat down in that room.

The night before the dialogue, those who would attend gathered at the home of a victim's advocate – and a friend of Leigh's – who had offered up her home as a meeting venue. Leigh had made a few of these acquaintances over the years: people who showed up to help and became like family. Tania Koen was one such person.

Tania is an attorney who describes herself as a workaholic and dedicates her spare time to helping the families of victims of crime navigate the legal system. She has supported Reeva Steenkamp's parents as well as the family of Leigh Matthews, who was kidnapped and murdered in 2004, and now she supports the victims of the Sizzlers massacre in their efforts to keep Adam Woest in prison.

"People don't get the help they need," Tania says. "I think there should be education for victims so that they can know what they can do." She adds, "Yes, the Matthews and Steenkamp families have had guidance, but the man in the street is not afforded the same privilege."

This sentiment must be acknowledged. If well-resourced victims and survivors are struggling to navigate the system, what of those who are disadvantaged, living in poverty and unable to access resources? Do they have any chance of being a voice for their murdered loved ones?

By the time the family members gathered around the dinner table the night before the dialogue, Tania had done her level best to prepare them for what was coming. Unfortunately, there was a wild card that could upset the apple cart: Adam Woest.

Despite her initial misgivings, Leigh describes the dialogue as one of the "single most empowering experiences of my life". As Woest shuffled into the boardroom that had been assigned to them, she immediately noticed that he looked at least 20 years older than his actual age – nothing like the image she'd had of him in her head, nor the one that had haunted her nightmares.

The dialogue would take eight to nine hours. It was emotionally exhausting for everyone present. Psychologists and social workers from the department attended to facilitate the conversation only when needed. The key to a successful dialogue is for the conversation to flow naturally. All parties should feel they can speak their minds, and Leigh felt this was achieved.

Woest was given the opportunity to start the dialogue with anything he wanted to say to the victims. Ordinarily, this would be the point at which an offender would express their remorse and explain their actions, and perhaps say what they have done in the ensuing years to rehabilitate themselves. Woest did none of that. Eventually, almost three hours in, one victim asked whether he would ever say "sorry". He still hadn't said it. That was when Woest showed his true colours. He frowned at the victim. "Of course I said I'm sorry. That's the first thing I said. I've been saying that all along!" Everyone at the table exchanged amazed glances. "No, Adam, you haven't said it once." Social workers eventually had to steer the conversation away from this point because Woest was adamant he had expressed his remorse, while everyone present knew he hadn't. His strange behaviour didn't stop there, though.

At one point, Leigh says, he explained that he had asked other inmates who had undergone the dialogue process for guidance on how best to represent himself. Later in the conversation, one victim asked him for clarification, wondering why he didn't just tell the truth and express his remorse. Surely that would be the best way to represent himself? To everyone's amazement, Woest denied having said that he had taken advice from other inmates. This happened on several more occasions throughout the dialogue. According to Leigh, he would make a statement and then deny he'd said it a few minutes later. Even the departmental staff were glancing at one another in confusion.

With each lie, though, Leigh felt more emboldened. As the minutes ticked by, she felt more and more of her own power – and perhaps her brother's power – returning to her. The monster who had haunted her dreams was a complete mess.

"Have you done the therapy they asked you to do, Adam?" Leigh asked. "For your mental health conditions? What's the status on that?"

A moment of silence followed her question. Woest clearly hadn't expected it. The mask slipped briefly, and then he turned to Leigh and replied, "No, they don't give me access to psychologists here."

An audible gasp came from the psychologists and social workers in the room. They clearly disagreed. But Woest was not finished. "It's not a problem, though, because at my last appointment with a therapist, she gave me the all-clear and said I could be released." The departmental staff, left speechless, could only stare down at the desk.

Leigh asked Woest to give them the name of that therapist, so she could follow up on the matter, but Woest quickly changed the subject.

Woest's statements to Leigh are blatantly untrue for the following reasons. First, although the department's own psychology team is short-staffed, the Kgosi Mampuru II Correctional Facility is well-known for its excellent complement of psychologists. In fact, it is likely to be part of the reason Woest was moved there from Pollsmoor in the Western Cape after he was diagnosed. The department has its failings, but in the experience of many sources, no offender with a diagnosed and treatable mental health condition is denied mental health services. Treatment is always the offender's choice, however, as no form of psychotherapy will be beneficial unless the patient is engaged and willing.

Second, departmental psychologists do not have it in their mandate to make statements such as giving someone "the all-clear". A psychologist's report is part of the departmental process for parole, but it does not make determinations about whether the offender is cleared for release. Any departmental psychologist making such a statement would be guilty of misconduct. Their role is to report to the parole board about the offender's mental health condition, whether they require additional treatment and whether from a psychological perspective there is a high risk of reoffending – if the offender has violent ideation or any sexual deviance. From there, the parole board makes a determination.

Woest's constant lying was strange and infuriating for the victims. Two moments in particular would horrify them beyond belief.

The first was when Woest admitted that he'd had a deep desire to kill long before he took nine lives at Sizzlers. He told the victims that he had fantasised about it since he was a child being bullied at school. Having dropped this bombshell, he said he was ready to admit why he had really committed the crimes. If a room could collectively hold its breath, this one did. This was, after all, what they had come for. Remorse would have been nice, but it was secondary to hearing the truth. Unfortunately, once again Woest's version of the truth proved flexible.

"I was a vigilante," he announced, pausing dramatically. "I believed those men had been doing bad things to children, and that is why I killed them. I realise now that I was wrong about that, but at the time, it made sense."

With all the air sucked out of the room, everyone present realised that these lies were all they would get from Woest. Perhaps the only truth he had shared was when he admitted he'd wanted to kill for a long time before he and Trevor walked into Sizzlers. He hadn't needed a reason.

Quinton Taylor echoes Leigh's sentiments about the victim–offender dialogue being empowering. It didn't quite have the intended outcome, but it felt good, he says, to sit there with all these people who had his back and fire questions at Woest. He enjoyed having the upper hand.

"I wanted to show him he hadn't won," Quinton says. "I wanted him to look at me and see that I am healthy and I am happy and I get to live my life in the outside world, and he has to stay locked up. I wanted to show him he tried to take my life, but it was actually his own that he took."

Nine hours after they arrived, Quinton and the group of emotionally and physically depleted family members left the prison. They may not have got many honest answers out of Woest, but, in a way, that was the greatest truth of all. Now they knew they had to keep fighting his parole with everything they had. He could not be unleashed on society.

Chapter 31

The sex worker

NJ Hourquebie knows exactly how young men and women find themselves in the sex trade, because it happened to him.

Like Quinton Taylor, NJ started doing male-on-male sex work to avoid homelessness. "I had my first client on my 20th birthday," he says – and, in his characteristic no-nonsense manner, he adds, "To be honest, I kind of liked it."

NJ says he viewed sex work like hairdressing, "which tends to annoy hairdressers".

"It was a service. Guys would come in and they weren't feeling very loved. They weren't feeling very attractive. They weren't feeling very wanted. And for an hour, I would give them my undivided attention. And they were everything. They had my complete focus. When they left, they felt confident and cared for. They felt loved. You could see the change. They'd walk in all slouched and they'd walk out feeling good about themselves."

At first, he worked from an establishment in Norwood and says that, although he knew the sex trade could be violent and dangerous, most of his clients were really nice people. NJ estimates that more than half of his clientele were married men who presented as straight in the outside world. They came to him to be themselves for a little while, and he was happy, at least at the time, to be that person for them. Of course, the money didn't hurt. "I was making absolute bundles of money. And most of it was getting used on partying and getting high."

After years of therapy, NJ now realises that he was getting rid of the money because it felt dirty to him. He would never become financially stable with sex work because the hidden psychological cost was far too high.

"At the time, I thought it was awesome!" he says. But it didn't take long for him to realise that "selling his body", as he puts it, had deeply damaged his psyche. Now in his forties, he still struggles with the idea of a healthy sexual relationship with anyone.

He found many aspects of the sex trade dehumanising. "They had what they would call hit-and-runs, which was like 15- to 20-minute sessions," he explains, "and a fishbowl where all the sex workers would sit in this glass room naked and the client would choose which one they wanted."

After spending a few years in the Johannesburg sex trade, NJ, like so many of the Sizzlers victims, decided that Cape Town was the place to be. "I lasted two days," he says. "The Cape Town scene was brutal. The gangs were moving into Sea Point, and the places where the gangs weren't in charge were mostly run by some really bad guys."

He says the street gangs at the time mostly involved themselves in the heterosexual sex trade. He didn't work at Sizzlers, only because he left soon after some bad experiences. Had he stayed a little longer, he knows he may have ended up there too.

By the time he gave Cape Town a second chance in 2004, there had been a "seismic shift in the scene, and security was through the roof".

As he was part of the LGBTQ+ community and the sex-work industry, NJ saw the impact of the Sizzlers massacre from both perspectives. He describes Sizzlers as the South African queer community's "Pulse nightclub shooting". It clearly changed how safe queer people felt. "I find it sad that so many of the younger queer generation don't even know about Sizzlers. We should remember these victims and what they went through."

In the same breath, NJ points out that he doesn't automatically assume all the victims of Sizzlers were queer. Just as so many of his clients were straight presenting in the outside world, he'd met many male sex workers who were straight. In the industry, a straight man offering male-on-male sex services is called "gay for pay". "For some reason, that is actually quite attractive to a lot of clients. The straight guys earn a lot of money."

Although NJ never worked for Aubrey Otgaar, he had heard through the industry grapevine that he was one of the few respectable establishment owners who didn't exploit his workers. He recalls that the camaraderie between the workers was always strong. "We would always stick together. Whether we were standing up against an exploitative boss or a violent customer, even if we bitched between ourselves occasionally, you knew the other guys had your back."

This bond extended to the outside world too. "Because you are looked down on so much by the general public, sometimes even your family, people in the industry become all you have," he says. "It's also really hard as a sex worker to have a relationship with someone who isn't in the industry, so we all ended up dating each other too."

NJ says that he was not surprised to hear that a minor – Stephanus Fouché – had been among the victims. "It was very common to have minors in these places. I've seen guys as young as 15 in the sex trade," he says, "and as an older guy you just protect them because you know from your own experience that they've probably come from something far worse, and at least they are safe and you can watch over them."

When the police raided the establishments where they worked, NJ and his fellow workers would hide the underage workers in cupboards or washing baskets. "Sometimes the cops would just let it slide. Maybe they also know that it's probably worse for them in the system than in the trade."

He clarifies that he knows it was the wrong thing to do, and that those boys were probably also psychologically damaged, but "sometimes you just do what you need to do to survive and worry about the consequences later".

Another thing that didn't surprise NJ about the aftermath of the Sizzlers crime was the confusion about the victims' names. "Everyone in the sex trade uses a pseudonym," he says, "and it's weird, but guys who used certain types of names seemed to get more business, like boys with Afrikaans names had to use an English-sounding name if they wanted to get customers."

The Sizzlers case has never really left NJ's mind. Being part of the queer community, his past as a sex worker and having been in Sea Point just before it all happened mean that he's always felt oddly connected to it. Today, NJ works as a content creator, virtual assistant and podcaster. On his podcast, *A Crime Most Queer*, he covered the Sizzlers case in four in-depth episodes.

There's another reason NJ still thinks about Sizzlers, and that is because he, like most others, doesn't believe the full truth was ever told. During media coverage of the case, NJ heard a name mentioned that sent shivers down his spine: Jason Myers (not his real name).

"The minute I heard him talking on the radio, I felt sick. I worked for him for a few years in Johannesburg. Jason being in the orbit of this case did not sit right with me."

Chapter 32

Hate crime, robbery or deadly message?

While there is no doubt that a robbery took place at 7 Graham Road, it is difficult to believe, given all the evidence, that this was the sole motive and that things just went badly wrong. Several theories have been touted over the years. Leigh Visser would love to know the truth, but she sometimes feels the conspiracy theories just detract from the most important parts of the case: the victims and keeping Woest behind bars.

All kinds of conjecture can arise in cases with this much mystery around them, so perhaps the most responsible thing to do is to analyse some of these theories and put them to bed.

The gang theory

Although many believed that the Sizzlers massacre was a message sent by a gang to warn other sex-establishment owners not to cross them by impeding on their territory or not paying protection money, the theory holds little water on closer inspection.

Neither Adam Woest nor Trevor Theys had any gang affiliations. Street gangs like the Hard Livings who were involved in the heterosexual sex trade in Sea Point at the time were not showing any interest in the gay sex trade. Street gang hits are also usually carried out by gang members or hitmen for hire, not in the way Woest and Theys carried out this crime.

A police officer who was not involved in the investigation claimed that the crime carried the hallmarks of the 28s prison gang. Significantly more knowledge about the 26s, 27s and 28s has been gleaned in the past 20 years, so criminologists understand their modus operandi far better now – but even then, this officer was the only one who thought the 28s could be involved. Murders committed by 28s members are undoubtedly ruthless and vicious. Some of the most gruesome murders committed in the Western Cape are by 28s-affiliated offenders, but a 28s crime will not be committed by anyone other than a 28s member. The Numbers gangs in general are closed off from outsiders and only admit new members who have been in prison. A 28s leader would not order a middle-aged taxi driver and a young white restaurant server with no criminal history to commit a massacre.

Much of the gang theory was driven by mistaken sightings reported in the media and claims that four men had been involved. These men were allegedly working for a drug syndicate in the area, and they were looking for two former Sizzlers workers who had stolen drugs from them. The claims were that the three-hour torture session had been aimed at gleaning information from the workers about the whereabouts of the stolen drugs and the thieves. Although this theory gained traction for a while, we can put it to bed because we have an eyewitness, Quinton Taylor, who knows there was no one else except Woest and Theys in the house that night. The victims were also not questioned about the whereabouts of anyone else or about drugs and money.

The gang theory, in all its different versions, does not stand up to the evidence.

The call

One piece of evidence that drove much of the speculation about a third party being involved in the crime was the phone call Quinton Taylor told the court he had heard Woest making. Neither the SAPS nor the prosecution presented any further evidence to prove or refute this during the trial, so it became part of the legend that surrounded the case. Who was the person on the other side of that call? The answer may be simple and not at all salacious: no one, because now-retired Detective Captain Jonathan Morris says there was no call. As part of the investigation, he says, he checked Woest's and Theys's phones, and they had made no phone calls while they were at the scene of the crime.

Woest had been wary of using his phone. After all, he'd used a pay phone in the street to call Sizzlers to set up the appointment – clearly already considering a future police investigation. Cellphone activity often trips offenders up, even today when it is well known that the SAPS can access such data. In 2003, these capabilities would have been less advanced, and it's impossible to say whether the SAPS would have been able to access information that had been deleted. Woest was arrested 24 days after the crime. That gave him ample time to delete call records from his phone. The most popular phone at the time, the Nokia 6600, already had the capability to clear logs. In fact, it had to be done regularly as cellphones then did not have much memory capacity. Of course, the SAPS could have pulled call records from the service provider.

In addition, Quinton Taylor would have had no idea if Woest made a call or received one. If his phone was on silent mode, it wouldn't have rung. Quinton would only have heard Woest talking and perhaps assumed he'd made the call. Again, the official SAPS position – at least from the retired investigating officer's point of view – is that there is no evidence to support the existence of a phone call, or at least not a call on Woest's or Theys's cell phones. There was, however, a landline installed at 7 Graham Road. The police docket does not deal with the landline records, but one person claimed that they had phoned Sizzlers that morning around 2am – so, right in the midst of the torture. That man was Jason Myers.

"Jason"

"Jason" is the name this individual used in the sex trade. He was a gay man who had run several sex-trade establishments in Johannesburg and, after developing a poor reputation there, moved to Cape Town to try his hand in the Mother City. It would emerge that even the name he supplied as his real name was not, in fact, the one on his birth certificate. He had inexplicably changed both his name and surname legally in 1994 – some believe to escape a dark past.

Jason's name pops up regularly in reporting on the Sizzlers case. One might say he "inserted himself into the investigation". None of Detective Jonathan Morris's notes list him as a person of interest, but for someone who wasn't involved, he seemed to have an awful lot to say about the case.

One reason Jason had left Johannesburg, and possibly changed his name, was because he wanted to get into politics. He had started an LGBTQ-focused party and was registering it with the Independent Electoral Committee. Of course, with sex work still illegal in South Africa, a candidate of a party on the voting roll could not be linked to the sex trade. So, it is believed that while Jason actually maintained his business interests in several sex-trade establishments in Johannesburg, he cut public ties with the industry. He also went on the offensive against the industry in Cape Town, accusing establishment owners of exploiting members of the queer community.

Jason's future political career was on thin ice, even in Cape Town. A newspaper journalist from Johannesburg had dug up information on him while he was still in that province, and Jason's life was the source that just kept on giving. Besides his involvement in the sex trade, he had allegedly been investigated by police for involvement in producing child-abuse images. He'd also been accused of blackmailing people who had purchased the images and videos from him.

By the time Jason had settled in Cape Town, he was doing everything he could to rebrand his budding political party. He made false claims to journalists about the party having 60,000 members. Although he was the only one running the party at the time, he made up personas for an entire portfolio of ministers. He was caught out by a journalist when he pretended to be the party's media liaison, "David Baxter". This was an alias he had used in the past, too. But before this lie was exposed, Jason's party encouraged what the media would later call the "blood wars" in the LGBTQ+ community. He publicly encouraged gay men to lie on blood-donation screening forms to protest against the discriminatory questions asked on the forms at the time (sexual orientation is no longer a screening question for blood donation).

Another alias of Jason's that was also exposed by a journalist was "Neil Watson". Under this name, he created a website that spread clickbait and fake news articles making exaggerated claims about the crime rate in South Africa. The website also engaged in race baiting and seemed to be solely aimed at spreading fear and misinformation. When it was taken down following a campaign launched by another politician, a new website took its place. The new site claimed to out 34 high-profile men for using gay sex workers. The politician who had gone up against Jason was on the list.

Jason's shady reputation in the sex industry included claims that he would regularly take photographs and videos of clients and use those to extort money from the men. This was frowned upon in both the sex industry and the LGBTQ+ community.

Although Jason could change his name to escape his past, he couldn't change his fingerprints – and one reporter figured out that he had been a suspect in a murder in Kroonstad, where he had briefly worked in a prison.

Jason had not gone to trial for that murder, which remains unsolved.

When the bombings at the Bronx, Blah Bar and other establishments and tourist attractions occurred in Cape Town, Jason used these to increase the visibility of his political party. He inflated victim numbers when interviewed by the press and inserted himself into the conversation at every opportunity.

As January 2003 loomed, Jason was doing everything he could to get his name out there. He feuded with several LGBTQ+ businesses and organisations in Sea Point – including Sizzlers. Jason accused Aubrey Otgaar of many unproven things – exploiting his workers, creating child-abuse images and extorting money from clients. Interestingly, these were all things Jason himself had been accused of in the past. It was a first for Aubrey, though. His reputation in the industry had been nothing but stellar, and he wasn't taking the accusations lying down. In December 2002, Jason reported Aubrey to the City of Cape Town for operating a business without a licence, but there was no immediate response to the complaint due to the impending festive season.

It seemed clear to many, in retrospect, that Jason was trying to shut down Sizzlers permanently – not because he had any moral qualms about it, but because he wanted to siphon off the Sizzlers trade. The political scene wasn't working out for him, and he was running out of money.

After the massacre, Jason was quickly on the scene to claim personal connections to the victims. Ever the saviour, he told journalists and police that the young men working at Sizzlers had contacted him because they were afraid. Unfortunately, he claimed, he would never find out what they were afraid of, as they were killed before he could speak to them.

Jason also claimed that Warren Visser had contacted him on the evening of 19 January 2003 and asked if they could speak after his shift. He said Warren was afraid and needed help. They had agreed to speak at 2am, but when Jason called the landline, the person who answered did not say anything. There was just a long silence on the other end of the line, and then it went dead. He also tried Warren's cellphone, but it was turned off.

Once the rumours of the involvement of a third party emerged, Jason claimed to have information about this, too. He said that he had received a threatening phone call in the weeks before the massacre happened. Someone had mistaken him for the owner of Sizzlers and threatened his life. Sizzlers was a Sea Point institution and it was well known that Aubrey Otgaar was the owner, so this seemed strange. Jason also claimed that after the murders, a masked man had accosted him in his apartment and threatened to kill him. The man instructed him to leave Cape Town immediately, so he did.

Before Woest and Theys were even sentenced for the crimes, Jason was gone and stayed gone. In fact, there is no trace of him anywhere today, and no one seems to know whether he is alive or dead.

While this is an interesting story about a mysterious man, it is a stretch to assume that Jason was in any way involved in the Sizzlers massacre. It does, however, provide another explanation for the phone call Quinton Taylor swears he heard. Jason admitted calling the house while the killers were there. He said the phone was answered but no one spoke on the other side. If Warren Visser really had been afraid and wanted to have a private conversation with Jason, why would the main house phone be a good option? Had the police looked at the landline call logs (we don't know for sure whether they did, but it didn't make it into the pack of evidence), they would have checked all the numbers that had phoned Sizzlers between midnight and 3am. One of those numbers would have belonged to Jason. So, he either really called to speak to Warren or had to explain the call before the police found it.

Jason may well have been nothing more than an unscrupulous man out to cause chaos and raise the profile of his soon-to-be-defunct political party. One thing brings him back into the picture, though: his address. Jason Myers lived in the Bordeaux apartment block, right next door to Adam Woest.

Hate crime

The worst-case scenario theory for Sea Point's LGBTQ+ community is that the Sizzlers massacre was a hate crime – defined as "a crime, typically one involving violence, that is motivated by prejudice on the basis of ethnicity, religion, sexual orientation or similar grounds".

This was all but ruled out during the trial, as the psychiatric reports on both men cleared them of having homophobic tendencies. Yet, Quinton Taylor says he felt plenty of aggression and what he interpreted as hatred from Adam Woest. In a throwaway comment that may hold some truth, Quinton adds that he doesn't know whether Woest really was homophobic or "maybe he had some tendencies of his own he didn't want to admit".

Although the Sizzlers massacre does not seem to be a blatant hate crime in the standard sense, there could still be an element of truth in that.

There is something else that has never been explained. Why, if Aubrey Otgaar knew both Adam Woest and his fiancée, Adele, was he so comfortable with the ruse that Woest used to get into the house that night – that he was there, with Trevor, to have a threesome with another man? Surely, if Aubrey knew Woest to be straight, he would have expressed some surprise when Woest came looking for the services of a male sex worker? But he didn't. He acted like he knew Woest, Quinton said, but it seemed normal that Woest would be there for a gay sexual liaison. A possible explanation is that Woest didn't know the Sizzlers workers and Aubrey just from the restaurant where he worked; perhaps he also knew them more intimately, as a client of Sizzlers.

Adele van den Heever mentioned no suspicions about Adam being gay or even bisexual. There's also no sign that she, as a heterosexual woman, would have been okay with Woest engaging in gay sex outside their relationship.

Adele was the main breadwinner in the household. She was young, bright and beautiful. Her work as a nursing aide brought in decent money, and she mostly paid for their apartment. She also owned the couple's only vehicle. Adam Woest had a good life with Adele, and perhaps he didn't want that to end. There was every chance that it would have ended if she'd discovered he was gay or bisexual and paying for sex.

It was no coincidence that the crime was committed the day after Adele left for Johannesburg. That was undoubtedly planned by Woest. So, what else did he do when Adele wasn't around? He worked late nights and it would not have been difficult for him to stop at Sizzlers on his way home and then, later, cross the road to his apartment.

Adam Woest admitted that he had always wanted to commit murder. He came up with the bizarre vigilante story during the victim–offender dialogue – an unlikely tale, given that it would have come up in his psychiatric assessment, but it may still contain a grain of truth.

Perhaps Woest had always wanted to commit murder, and perhaps he was hiding his sexuality from the world. Even though his own brother was gay and he seemed to not be outwardly homophobic, he still may not have wanted that to get out because he feared losing Adele.

One of the mental health conditions – a personality disorder – that Woest was eventually diagnosed with presents with significant paranoia as a prominent feature. Perhaps he'd started to think his secret was not safe with Aubrey and decided to make his fantasy a reality while also wiping out everyone who knew about his sexuality.

It would certainly explain the torture and the aggression, and it would explain why Aubrey was comfortable with the idea of Woest being a customer. The only thing it does not explain is why Woest and Theys spent three hours in the house, and Quinton Taylor's feeling that Woest was waiting for something or someone.

The two men got all the valuables early into the three-hour period. Yet, Quinton said, Woest kept searching and ransacking rooms. Photographs of Aubrey Otgaar's room show all his belongings pulled out and rifled through. Woest could have been looking for more money or valuables, of course, but that still wouldn't have covered three hours. If he was looking for something else, though – a specific item or items – it might explain his strange behaviour.

This is where Woest's neighbour, Jason Myers, might come in. In the weeks before the massacre, Jason had accused Aubrey of many terrible things, including taking photographs and videos of his clients to extort them.

Woest is not necessarily an easily led person. After all, he took the lead in the massacre and filled the role pretty well. He is manipulative, with all the hallmarks of a dangerously unempathetic personality. But everyone has their weak spots, and if Woest's Achilles heel was his desire to keep his sexuality a secret, hearing from his neighbour that Aubrey had photographs and video of his clients could very well have been a huge contributing factor to his decision to kill.

To be clear, Aubrey was not extorting anyone. He had not secretly taken videos or photographs of anyone. But Woest didn't know that. Perhaps he was looking for the photos and the videos, and maybe the 2am phone call from Jason was pre-planned and a mid-point check-in. Quinton couldn't hear what Woest was saying, but he could have been saying, "I can't find any photos or videos."

Trevor Theys seemed convinced that it was only a robbery. He had to have known they would kill people too, but he may have decided it was worth it or convinced himself it might not happen. He didn't seem to understand why Woest was hanging around, either. If Woest was looking for photos or videos he thought were in the house, he also couldn't have asked Aubrey outright because Theys would have heard.

Whether Jason did somehow influence Woest into

committing the crime, intentionally or unintentionally, or whether Woest came up with the paranoid thoughts all on his own does not in any way detract from his guilt.

Rather, it almost makes it worse. If he committed these murders to keep his own secret, thinking he would get away with it and score some extra cash – and if he kept his secret even after his life blew up in his face – he is even more dangerous than originally thought.

There is no doubt that Detective Jonathan Morris caught the right men, and Leigh Visser is correct – debating theories does detract from the most important parts of this case. Thankfully, the evidence seems to have put paid to most of these theories. Except one.

Chapter 33

The present

The detective

When now-retired Detective Jonathan Morris joined the SAPS in the 1970s, he was issued a decrepit Smith & Wesson revolver because he was coloured. His white colleagues each received three brand-new, high-calibre weapons. As the white student constables strolled out of the station at the end of their shifts with their 9mm Parabellums, shotguns and R1 rifles, Morris and his fellow coloured constables queued to hand back their weapons. They weren't allowed to take their service revolvers home with them. SAPS top brass seemed to have decided that levels of trustworthiness were determined by the colour of a recruit's skin.

Although apartheid would officially fall in South Africa 17 years after Morris had joined the SAPS, he navigated discrimination throughout his career. He doesn't openly bear a grudge, though. Rather, he is proud of his rise through the ranks to become one of the SAPS's finest despite having dealt with absurd inequality in the foundational phase of his career.

Morris's career could have gone either way. As a student officer, he was exposed to both the best and the worst the police service (a "force" in those days) had to offer in terms of leadership. After witnessing a senior officer, inebriated on duty, shoot an unarmed, 15-year-old prisoner in the holding cells after kicking the boy awake, the young constable drew a line in the sand. By refusing to cover for that officer and instead testifying against him (which led to the senior officer's dismissal and conviction on criminal charges), Morris showed the world what type of police officer he would be. He developed a reputation for being hard-headed and unfazed by the bullying tactics of some of his superiors. Along the way, he also met police officers he looked up to – men and, later in his career, women who exemplified the ethics he felt were required to wear the uniform with pride.

Morris remembers the first murder scene he attended. A young man, known in the neighbourhood as "Liefling", was killed in a street gang fight between the Mongels and the Laughing Boy Kids. The victim, a member of the latter gang, was hacked to death by several panga-wielding Mongels members. It was the first of many murder scenes in Morris's career. He joined the detective branch not long after, officially qualified with his diploma from the police college, and never looked back. His knack for solving a mystery quickly became apparent to his superiors, and on countless occasions he would be called upon to solve the seemingly unsolvable.

Morris's memory is a terrifying Rolodex of offender names, gruesome injuries and victims for whom he sought justice. Within that index is a case that is closer to home than any other – his own son. Morris explains that his son went down a path he'd tried to steer him away from – and so his child was caught up in a web of hard drugs. The young man was shot dead in a tavern, and the case remains unsolved to this day. "Because they wouldn't let me work on it," he says, by way of explanation, with a wink and a wry, sad smile.

Many of the murder scenes Morris worked on are still fresh in his mind decades later. He can describe some in great detail, but what he found in that house on Graham Road, Sea Point, still makes the words catch in his throat. He is clearly incredibly proud of the work he did on this case, and he should be. With his police career now behind him, he rarely has occasion to talk about the cases he worked on. Most are not exactly dinner-table conversation.

Morris talks about Quinton Taylor with reverence. He knows all too well that without Quinton, things may have gone very differently. He speaks of Leigh Visser with a fond smile, too. They've never met, but there is an undeniable bond between the two: the man who hunted monsters and the young woman who wants to keep one behind bars.

Morris has retired to a small fishing village in the Western Cape. Now, he spends his mornings walking the beach instead of crime scenes. His neighbours have no idea they have a national hero living next door. Policing never leaves the bloodstream, though, and Morris admits he's still on one or two WhatsApp groups that keep him updated on what's happening in the world of crime. The difference is that he can now read the message and switch off his phone. It's not his responsibility anymore.

His eyes twinkle with a surge of adrenaline as his body remembers while he talks about his career. After Sizzlers, he specialised in gang-related cases and eventually cash-in-transit heists and ATM bombings. The memories spill from his mouth as he looks out over the ocean. Every time the conversation turns back to that scene at Graham Road, something changes, ever so slightly, in his eyes. It's an almost imperceptible darkening. The knowledge, perhaps, that on that day, he witnessed something that changed him.

Leigh

When Leigh Visser walked out of the victim–offender dialogue in January 2023, she left her demons behind with Adam Woest. "I can't really explain it," she says, "but I don't have those nightmares anymore." She didn't realise it immediately. After spending a few more weeks with her family in South Africa, she flew back to her husband in Canada. It was only once she was back home that she realised the panic attacks were gone. "It's almost like the power I'd given him over me dissipated when I saw how ... pathetic ... he was." She almost immediately apologises for using the word to describe anyone, even a mass murderer, but that's how she feels.

Leigh hasn't heard from the Department of Correctional Services since the dialogue was held. She assumes a parole hearing will be held at some point, but she has been unable to get any information about when that will happen. Tania Koen has also been trying to get information, to no avail. Queries to the department for this book also went unanswered. What Leigh does know is that offenders are usually given a parole hearing every two years. So, this is not the end of the fight. It's likely to be only the beginning.

For 20 years, Leigh Visser did not tell anyone who entered her life how her brother died – not because she was ashamed or felt it was something she should hide, but because she didn't want it to define her. She tried to put Woest and Theys in a box and hoped they would stay there. All she wanted was to live a normal life in her new home in a new country and forget that Sizzlers ever happened. She didn't want to forget her brother, Warren, though; just the way he died. But Woest and the way the department handled his possible parole made that impossible. They made Leigh choose: justice for her brother and the other victims, or the normal life she wanted to live. So, she chose to get involved, because, she says, "He would have done the same for me."

Quinton

As part of a therapeutic process, Quinton Taylor has written a book about his experience at Sizzlers, his life before that and his journey to becoming the man he is today. His hope is that one day it will inspire many people. He lived in Johannesburg for a long time, out in the mountains, where there is little phone signal and few people. He worked at a guest house for many years and came to love the hospitality industry. Now, he lives in Cape Town and is setting up an Airbnb with a friend.

He is excited to see that more countries are allowing South Africans in without visas, and he's already got a few places on his bucket list. Working as a carer in the UK is one idea he's been toying with. He'll see, though. Life is a journey. For now, he's enjoying the ride.

Quinton and Leigh started chatting by text before the victim–offender dialogue and are still in touch. He is incredibly protective of her and the other family members. His friends aren't here to protect them anymore, after all.

Although he has put the fear of that night behind him, he admits that his worst nightmare is one day walking through a shopping centre and seeing Adam Woest. If the parole board decides Woest is cleared for release, that nightmare might not be too far off.

Epilogue

In February 2024, to the best of our knowledge, Adam Roy Woest remains detained at Kgosi Mampuru II Correctional Facility. The department has still not provided the families or their representatives with any information regarding the next steps in his parole review.

The family members of the victims of the Sizzlers massacre need support in their plight to keep Woest behind bars. This is not a quest for vengeance. No amount of prison time will give back what has been taken from them. Rather, it is a desire to ensure the public is protected from a man who ruthlessly murdered nine men, tried to kill a tenth and then lied about it for decades.

Leigh Visser does not want to be a public figure, but that horse has bolted. So, in exchange for the life she'd thought she would have, she asks only for the support of South African citizens who see fit to do so. Her online petition is still live, and every signature will bring her closer to her goal.

This book has also sought to bring clarity to the challenges in our parole system. For additional information on the current state of our parole system as well as proposed changes, please see the "additional information" section at the end of this book.

We should all understand and work towards making the system better for everyone. Tomorrow, it could be your family.

The position, of course, is not that parole in itself is a bad thing. It is not. Parole is a necessary and important part of our justice and correctional system. Many horror stories exist about poor parole decisions, but there are also many uplifting stories about offenders who have been rehabilitated – even after murdering someone. The average citizen may be surprised to learn how many people who are now successful members of society committed violent crimes in their past. The one thing all these rehabilitated offenders have in common, though, is that they admitted the full extent of their crimes and showed themselves, warts and all, to the world, so that they could heal. Most of them also did not kill nine people.

Although the families of the offenders have not specifically been mentioned in this book, their unique pain is acknowledged. The Woest and Theys families have committed no crimes. One member of each of their families did, and it is with those two men that the shame of this horrendous act belongs.

Acknowledgments

To Melinda Ferguson: Somehow you always take what I think is mediocre drivel and turn it into something closely resembling a good book. You are a magician. I know you go far above and beyond what is ordinarily offered by a publisher, and I am incredibly grateful. No matter where our paths take us, you will always be the person who made six-year-old Nicole's dream come true. You make me a better writer and I couldn't be prouder to call you my publisher. Thank you for the opportunities you've given me and for being willing to give a voice to these victims.

To Leigh Visser: I can never thank you enough for trusting me. I hope I got the balance right and that you feel like this book is a positive way for Warren to be remembered. When your descendants look back at you, they will see the incredibly fierce warrior that you are, and they will know that his strength lives on in you and them.

To Quinton Taylor: It was an incredible privilege to meet you and see how happy and healthy you are now. You took your power back. I promise you, you will never be on your own in this fight.

To Detective Captain Jonathan Morris: there is no way I could have written this book without you. I wish every police officer in our country had your integrity and passion. Enjoy your retirement. You've earned it.

Dr Hestelle van Staden, thank you so much for your support, kind words of encouragement, and keen eye. While it's always handy having a forensic pathologist on WhatsApp, you mean far more to me. I am very proud to call you a friend.

To every other person who took me into their confidence and contributed to this book, I hope I have represented you accurately. Thank you for still thinking of these victims so often. Each one of you played an integral role in helping me to tell this story. I am incredibly grateful.

Additional information

The need for parole reform

In theory, the South African parole system is not entirely broken. The restorative justice process and the idea of rehabilitative incarceration are both solid and world-class concepts, but as with some aspects of our robust Constitution, we fail in the application. The idea is there, but the execution is often dismal.

Many citizens believe that "life in prison" should mean a prisoner's entire life, but there are few countries in the world where this is true. Most prison systems are not built to house thousands of people for the rest of their natural lives. South Africa actually has one of the longest minimum incarceration periods in the world for life sentences. Many countries consider lifers for parole after 10 or 15 years. So, in that aspect, at least, we far exceed the international standard.

Questions about parole start when an offender is sentenced. South Africa's minimum sentencing structure has improved considerably over the years – out of necessity. The higher our crime rate got, the more we recognised that short sentences weren't helping. A big issue in our current sentencing structure is that judges do not have the ability to easily hand down a sentence in which an offender will never receive parole. Even though this type of sentence is rarely handed down, it can be appropriate in some cases. In the UK, for instance, a judge can hand down what is called a whole-life term.

In South Africa, our closest equivalent is the "dangerous offender" determination, which is not used nearly as often as it should be. An offender classed as "dangerous" does not have access to the ordinary parole system. Instead, when they would ordinarily become eligible for parole, they must appear before a judge again. The judge then weighs up their eligibility for release. This determination should be used much more often because our parole review system is fatally flawed. Most importantly, the individuals who sit on parole boards are often not qualified to decide whether an offender still poses a risk to society. Qualified psychologists and criminologists do submit reports to the board for consideration, but the actual decision is made by individuals who lack the appropriate experience. These have been reported to include administrative staff in the employ of the Department of Correctional Services and even church leaders.

The criteria used by the parole board to decide whether an offender should be released are also questionable. Remorse still features as an important criterion, as does good behaviour in prison. Considering that the most dangerous of offenders are also expert manipulators, it is easy for them to fake remorse – and, as Dr Gérard Labuschagne says, "It's easy to behave well in prison.

That's not an indication of how you are going to behave in the outside world."

Our parole system also fails to ensure that the parole board has access to all the relevant information about an offender's criminal history and the crime for which they were incarcerated.

This is one part of the Sizzlers case that baffled those involved. In passing down his sentence, Judge Nathan Erasmus stated, "Whilst the potential release of a prisoner may fall outside the court's domain, I am sure that the committee will have regard to the fact that life imprisonment, in my view, is not easily imposed but only in those cases where I am of the view that the accused should be permanently removed from society. I propose that the comments I make in this case be placed before any organ that may consider parole for the accused should it become necessary at a later stage."

Many who were present that day, and those reading a summary of the sentencing in the media, took this to mean Judge Erasmus was saying Woest and Theys should never be released on parole. This often happens in particularly violent cases and is misunderstood as an overriding ruling. In South Africa, judges do not have authority over offenders after they are sentenced unless they are officially categorised as dangerous offenders. While a judge can, as Judge Erasmus did, make recommendations to a future parole board, they cannot dictate whether an offender will be released. Judge Erasmus mentions in his sentencing that he hopes his remarks will be noted on the offenders' files and be read by a future parole board, but in many cases this does not happen.

Administrative issues and poor record-keeping often result

in little information about a crime and sentencing following an offender to their parole hearing. The longer the offender has served in prison, the more likely it is that not all the relevant information will be placed before the parole board.

This potential failure in the system is why many dangerous serial offenders are released back into society. If a parole board is not aware of the extent of an offender's crimes or their repeated recidivism (reoffending), they are at risk of judging suitability for release solely based on their status. This is like saying a car that hasn't broken down while idling in the garage is fit to take on a 1,000km road trip. If you don't know the car has a history of overheating every 100km, you're in for a bumpy ride.

When dealing with the psychological nature of a repeat or otherwise dangerous offender, this can be a fatal decision for their future victims – and has proved to be just that on many occasions.

It almost seems ludicrous to consider that a person with nine life sentences might be granted parole. In her petition, Leigh Visser asks for the way in which sentencing is handed down to be changed, including concurrent and consecutive sentencing. When offenders are sentenced for a single crime, even if there are multiple sentences attached to it, a judge will say they must be served concurrently. This means that, in Adam Woest's case, for instance, he serves all nine life sentences, as well as the additional years he got for the lesser charges, at the same time. The opposite would be if an offender has to serve their sentences consecutively – one after the other. In that case, the offender serves the first portion of their sentence and then begins the next. Consecutive sentencing is usually reserved for cases in which an offender has committed different and unrelated crimes at different times in their life. Even serial killers who commit murders with cooling-off periods in between are sentenced concurrently. This is because their crimes are all brought to trial at the same time and are seen as part of one series, not individual incidents.

Handing down consecutive sentences is difficult because such an order will usually be repealed on appeal, as it can be argued that it violates the offender's constitutional rights. Ordering an offender to serve multiple life sentences consecutively (even if they are related to separate incidents) can also easily be appealed, as an offender only has one natural life. Judges will sometimes sentence an offender to serve part of one sentence concurrently with part of another. They will then include in their sentencing a remark about what the effective sentence should be.

This does not happen with life sentences, though. Rather, the impact of multiple life sentences and the seriousness of such a sentence should be considered when the offender is eligible for parole. Of course, none of that helps the victims avoid having to spend much of the rest of their own lives attending parole hearings.

Herein lies the balance that needs to be maintained. Victims cannot stop parole from happening by objecting to it. They have only a partial influence on the parole process, but what cannot be calculated is the true impact of the absence of their objection. If victims in South Africa could trust parole boards to release only truly rehabilitated offenders, there would be less need for the pain of their continued involvement in the process. That is not the case. As a result, it is the family members and survivors who endure a true life sentence. They must follow up, attend hearings and raise objections until they (or the offender) die.

Of course, South Africa is not the only country in the world where parole is a contentious issue. Victims across the world report similar experiences. It's not a unique problem, but what makes our situation different is the frequency with which parole system failures occur.

Although the impact of the Van Wyk, Van Vuren and Phaala judgments on victims is devastating, they will not be reversed. Concurrent and consecutive sentencing rulings are also not likely to change. For those who believe the death penalty would be a solution, it would require a complete overhaul of entire sections of our Constitution, which is highly unlikely.

If beneficial change is to be enacted in the parole system in South Africa, it is more effective to focus on the most problematic areas that can be changed.

What can (and should) change?

Anyone who spends time dealing with victims of violent crime and their families will have horror stories to tell about how they have been re-victimised and terrorised by the system.

Debby Thomson's brother Mike was murdered in a home invasion in 2007. The gang of criminals had also committed many other violent crimes. Their case took almost a decade to move through the justice system, which is a serious issue in and of itself. After sentencing,

Debby wished to contact some of the offenders, but she hit a wall. Most worrying of all was that the Department of Correctional Services often didn't even know where the offenders were being held.

At the end of Leigh Visser's petition, she links another petition. It belongs to a woman she's befriended because they are dealing with shared trauma – the loss of a loved one to murder, followed by attempts to navigate the parole system. Roxanne van Eck was just 18 years old in 2003 when her father, Table View police officer Leslie Cilliers, was gunned down by a gang on the run from a bank robbery. Leslie was shot 52 times with a semi-automatic firearm. His killers were arrested and convicted, but they, like Woest, benefited from the Van Wyk judgment. After they had served just 18 years in prison, Roxanne was told that her father's murderers were eligible for parole. She experienced similar frustrations in trying to figure out what she had to do. With six offenders involved in her father's murder, Roxanne's nightmare is on a far greater scale than some of the other crimes mentioned here. Perhaps most terrifying is that the department still cannot tell Roxanne where some of the offenders in Leslie's case are, or even whether they are still incarcerated.

In 2006, 22-year-old Marlene Mauer was murdered by Daniel van der Walt after the man set up a fake job interview to lure the young woman to his home. He was sentenced to 17 years in prison after the judge found his drug use and a prior head injury may have contributed to his crime. In 2019, Marlene's mother received a message from a friend on Facebook asking her whether she knew Van der Walt was out of prison. The department had not informed Marlene's family that the offender was being considered for parole, and her right to submit an objection and take part in the process was violated. She has still had no response from the department to her queries.

Jerome Davids murdered his wife, Charmelin, in 2009. He was handed down a 25-year determinate sentence. In March 2023, Charmelin's brother heard from a friend that Jerome had been released on parole the month before. The department seemed to recognise its error after Charmelin's family complained. It made the parole null and void, and took Davids back into custody. This situation affected not just the victim's family but also the offender's family, who were distraught at having their family member taken back into custody without explanation.

These are just a small sample of the cases in which victims' families and survivors of violent crime are re-victimised by a frustrating and haphazard system. These victims also had access to resources. The stories of victims in disadvantaged communities are surely far worse.

We do not point out these failings to criticise the Department of Correctional Services. Rather, in acknowledging these instances, we must ask ourselves: if the simple terms of the Service Charter for Victims of Crime in South Africa are not being adhered to, what else is going wrong? With a recidivism rate of 50–90 percent in South Africa, we cannot afford to release offenders who are not ready to be safely integrated into society.

To understand where change can be effected, it's important to understand how the parole process is *intended* to work.

The process starts inside the prison about six months before the offender's first date of eligibility for parole. The prison's case management committee (CMC) manages the internal process. Whenever a positive or negative incident is recorded regarding the offender, it goes back to the CMC to collect these records for an eventual parole hearing. This includes reports from psychologists about ongoing therapy, certificates gained through the completion of rehabilitation programmes, skills training records, and any violations or notes about negative behaviour such as drug use or gang involvement.

Six months before the first parole hearing, the CMC will issue a notification to all stakeholders to prepare an offender profile. Departmental psychologists will also put together risk assessment reports using internationally approved, evidence-based criteria. Both static and dynamic factors are involved in this assessment. Static factors are facts about the offender and the crime that cannot change – their actions, their age at the time, details of the crimes and more. Dynamic factors relate to rehabilitation. Has the offender shown marked improvement in the types of behaviour that led them to the crime? Do they understand their actions? Do they know how to avoid repeating the mistakes that led them to prison?

The risk assessment is essentially a mini-investigation of the crime and the offender's role. It should include as much information as possible, including sentencing remarks, victim statements and even details from the original police docket.

Meanwhile, it is the job of departmental victim tracers to find the victims of the case, make contact, explain what is happening and offer the victims the opportunity to take part in a victim–offender dialogue and sit in on the parole hearing.

Once this is done and the date of eligibility nears, the offender parole profile is handed over to the Correctional Supervision and Parole Review Board (CSPB) to carry out the next part of the process. After a decision is reached through voting, it is sent to the National Council of Correctional Services for review and, in some instances, to the minister of correctional services for further review.

Victims have both rights and responsibilities in the parole process. According to the Service Charter for Victims of Crime in South Africa, victims of crime or their family members (in the case of murder) have the right to participate in a victim–offender dialogue. They also have the right to offer information or contributions of their choosing at a parole hearing, and to be supported by the department throughout the process. This support includes explaining everything to the victim or family member in a way they can understand.

Also, according to the charter, victims have the responsibility to inform the CSPB of their intention to participate in the parole review process in writing after they have been informed of the offender's eligibility. They also have to update their contact details with the CSPB when necessary.

Generally, if an offender is declined for parole, they will be reviewed again in 24 months.

It is clear, from the Sizzlers massacre and the other examples shared here, that this process does not always work the way it should. In addition, there are aspects of it that can be changed to be less frustrating for the victims.

The first point at which the system seems to fail is in tracing victims to inform them of the parole review and involve them in the victim–offender dialogue. Regardless of occupation, some people will go above and beyond in performing their duties while others will do the bare minimum or nothing at all. Human nature cannot be changed, but it is vital to hold accountable those victim tracers who are doing substandard work or even making false claims about what they have done.

However, the tracers face a lack of resources. While trying to locate her brother's murderers in prison, Debby Thomson found that the victim tracer assigned to her did not even have a working telephone and shared a desk with three other employees. Easily accessible online resources can help the tracers find victims and their families, but they need to be able to access them.

In reality, victim education is the most important part of all, and it should start long before the offender is eligible for parole. Far too often, victims and families misunderstand what a sentence means. Then, years down the line, the horrible reality sinks in. Although it is not part of the department's mandate, prosecutors would aid the process significantly if they took a few minutes to explain to the families what the sentence actually meant and what they could expect to happen in 20 or 25 years.

Once victims have been traced and the shock of discovering an offender is eligible for parole wears off, they are often confused about what they need to do. Despite the victim charter stating that they have a right to have the process explained to them, this does not always happen. Most often, victims are left to fend for themselves and find their own resources. Again, the people who do not provide the mandated service should be held accountable. If there is no penalty, their poor performance will simply continue.

Perhaps the most important and urgent change required in our parole system is at the parole-board level. Every member of the board must have a background in law, psychology, criminology, corrections or a closely related field. Given the complexity of the criminal mind, it cannot be left to individuals with degrees in education, for instance, or church leaders, to determine which offenders should be released.

Another important change, but one that may be difficult to implement, is extending the period between parole reviews for certain offenders. Certainly, in cases such as Adam Woest's where the offender has nine life sentences and there are substantial risk factors, it cannot be the best use of our resources to review such a parole application every two years – never mind the impact on the victims.

Finally, if an offender is released by a parole board and they reoffend, there should be accountability. Instances of violent offenders being released only to murder or rape again are reported regularly. In such cases, a mechanism to review the original parole board's decision and act against misconduct is vital. This is unlikely to happen through government channels; the only way such a change can be affected may be through sustained class-action suits by the many victims affected by poor parole-board decisions.

When asked about possible changes to our parole system, Department of Correctional Services spokesperson Singabakho Nxumalo intimated that a review of our parole system will be implemented "soon".

For the hundreds of thousands of South Africans negatively affected by these failings, "soon" is not good enough.

Sources

Morris, J. (2023). Sizzlers case investigation (N. Engelbrecht, interviewer) [Personal communication].

Visser, L. (2023). Warren Visser and Parole Experience (N. Engelbrecht, interviewer) [Personal communication].

Taylor, Q (2024). Life after Sizzlers (N. Engelbrecht, interviewer) [Personal communication].

Nevin, N (2024). Medic Response to Sizzlers (N. Engelbrecht, interviewer) [Personal communication].

Anonymous Source (DCS) (2024). Parole System Information. (N. Engelbrecht, interviewer) [Personal communication].

NJ Hourquebie (DCS) (2023). Life as a sex worker. (N. Engelbrecht, interviewer) [Personal communication].

Got Your Black supplied audio interviews: Elsabé Brits, Gérard Labuschagne, Quinton Taylor.

SAPS supplied statements, confessions, photographs, and other docket information.

Court judgment and sentencing document.

Brits, E. (2011). Kyk My in die Oë (1st ed.). Tafelberg.

Podcast – A Crime Most Queer – 4-part Sizzlers episode. NJ Hourquebie

Merten, M. (2003, January 31). Sea Point "unrecognisable" as gangs move in. The Mail & Guardian. https://mg.co.za/article/2003-01-31-sea-point-unrecognisable-as-gangs-move-in/

Viall, J. (2004, June 29). "I guess I never really knew him after all." IOL. https://www.iol.co.za/news/south-africa/i-guess-i-never-really-knew-him-after-all-215932

Abrahams, K. W. (2021, April 13). Ex-lover of Sizzlers victim pours out his heart: "No one knew him like I did." You. https://www.news24.com/you/news/local/ex-lover-of-sizzlers-victim-pours-out-his-heart-no-one-knew-him-like-i-did-20210413

https://www.change.org/p/petition-against-the-parole-of-mass-murderers-in-south-africa-warning-graphic